Unapologetically Grief: Raw and Real

A story of grief through sexual abuse, manipulation, suicide, and more

CL Smith, Author

D1622125

I knew several years ago that I needed to tell my story. I knew it would be painful and hard to open myself up to judgment and criticism. I already know I made a lot of mistakes. I don't need the reminders. So, why did I write this book? If my story resonates with or helps one person who is struggling to find their way through unimaginable grief, then it will be worth it to share my painful story. When dealing with things out of our control, it is easy to be blind to manipulation, even when we say it can never happen to us. It can. Believe me. I wish I could change the past, but I can't. I can't change what happened and I can't change how I responded to it. All I can do is share my story, continue to grow in my faith, continue to learn, and hopefully help others that are struggling.

This is my story and not my kids' stories. It is not my place to tell their complete stories. Our stories intercept and I tell how I responded to certain things they did but I am careful to try to not go into too much detail about the abuse or some of my youngest son's behaviors. I tried to balance what I felt was necessary for the story.

Disclaimer: I changed all the names in this book to protect the privacy of my kids and grandkids. I didn't want to change my ex-husband's name and I didn't do it to protect him, but I did it for my kids. He hurt my most precious things. I didn't change the names because we are trying to hide from the truth but to maintain some privacy for them as they still have grief and things to deal with.

I journaled a lot during that time and I have shared my journal entries that go along with the other parts of the story. They are in random order, but I wanted the entries to correlate with parts of the story. These journal entries were cries out to God. They were my raw, real grief and confusion.

There is probably a lot I could have added to this story, but my goal was to keep it short and easy to read. I wanted it to touch people who have experienced any kind of grief and for them to know that it is okay to feel grief and express grief.

Thank you for reading my story!

In memory of Josh:
My son, I love you

Chapter One: July 8, 2015

Eyes are the gateway to the soul
His are haunted and scared
The blue is diminished
By the pain of the truth.
Anchors are secured by chains of dread
Wrapping around his scrawny legs.
Each step painful.
Each step closer to sharing the pain.
His revelation leaves me blindsided
And changes the dynamics of all we love.
Remove those chains
Release the anchors
Son, let me be your anchor.

The old building didn't stay cool very well and I felt like little pieces of me were melting. Even my fan wasn't helping against the Missouri humidity and heat. But even the heat couldn't distract me from watching my son at the other desk. I didn't usually enjoy bringing an eleven-year-old to work, but I couldn't send him with my mom today, because he has had a horrible attitude, worse than a bear woken up from hibernation. I couldn't understand what had gotten into my son, but on this day, something seemed different.

I watched him over my computer, trying to decipher what was going on in that thick skull of his. He was slumped over his crossword puzzle, pencil in hand, giving me his familiar glare from under his St. Louis Cardinals ball cap. Nothing was unusual about any of that. He hated when he had to come to my office and not go with Grandma. Even though this seemed like his normal glare, something was wrong, something was different.

I tried to focus on my work. I worked for our small-town newspaper as a reporter and did the layout of the pages on the computer. The newspaper office was in an old building on the square, and it used to house a bank many years ago. When I decided to take a break from nursing and work at the paper, it was a big change. It was interesting learning about light tables and how a newspaper went together. We printed out the ads and articles, used a wax machine to make the paper stick to the design prints on the light table. Our boss used a large old printing press to print the pages. It was fascinating to learn how to do that, but a relief when we decided to use the computer to design the pages. The wax machine and other equipment were still in the building, almost like a museum.

I loved my job and appreciated the flexibility when I had to bring Michael with me on days like today. But, as much as I tried to focus on the task in front of me, I was distracted by my son's obvious despair.

Finally, Michael spoke. "I want to tell you something, but I can't."

"Why can't you?"

He looks up with fear in his eyes. "'Cause Dad told me I couldn't."

I was running through many possibilities in the few split seconds before I responded. My birthday was next week, so maybe Ray was planning a birthday surprise for me and shared it with the kids. I hoped that it was something similar to that, but I knew it wasn't. Why would Mike be scared if they were planning a birthday surprise?

"Son, you know you can tell me anything. What's wrong?"

"I can't tell you this, Mom. I just can't."

"Michael, come here."

He slowly got up from his chair and walked the ten feet to my desk, passing the old green wax machine on the other side of my desk. His posture was slouched, and his orange shorts were baggy on his scrawny frame. He was small for his age and the jacket he was wearing hung off him. We argued about the jacket this morning because it was a hundred degrees outside, but I finally decided the battle wasn't worth fighting. As he inched closer, it looked like each time he lifted a foot, it was painful to take the next step. As he came around my desk to my chair, I noticed that he was visibly shaken. My son was terrified. I was confused. This kid pushed all my buttons and at times drove me insane, but this look was one I had never seen before, and I felt my heart rate increase and pound in my ears.

"Michael, you're scaring me. What's wrong with you?"

He had difficulty speaking. "I'm not supposed to tell you, Mom. I can't. I'll be in trouble."

My worry went from the fifth floor to the penthouse in hearing those few words. I couldn't begin to imagine what he was talking about. Every mom instinct in me knew that something was not right. I watched as he put his head down and his shoulders sagged. It seemed like an eternity, but it was only a matter of seconds before he spoke. The words he said hit me like a freight train barreling across me. Time stopped, the world stopped, life stopped. I couldn't hear anything after those words.

I grabbed him and hugged him tight, and knew in my heart that our lives were about to be turned upside down. I kept replaying the words. "Dad made me do things. Bad things. Dad made me do them to him and he did them to me."

Ray and I were married on September 5, 1998. I was a single mom with two kids, a daughter, Lily, who was six, and Josh, who was three. My first marriage, in 1990, was a mess of two young people who had no clue. After discovering he had cheated on me, we divorced, and the kids and I started a new life. I wasn't in a hurry to get married again. A good friend of mine owned a beauty salon and that is where I met Ray. He would come into the salon and get his hair cut, and we barely spoke to each other. One time he came in dressed as the Easter Bunny and Josh was with me and excited to see the Bunny.

My friend ended up arranging our first date, which was her wedding. It didn't go well because he had a flat tire, and he didn't make it to the wedding and was late getting to the reception. I was standing behind the cake and food table and Ray, holding his daughter, came through the line. I offered to hold his daughter and he refused, saying they were going to go home. I didn't give it another thought and wrote the whole thing off. I found out later that he was upset about the flat tire and being late.

 A few days later, I received a message from him on my answering machine asking me on a date. On May 23, 1998, we went to a movie, *The Horse Whisperer*. My mom watched the kids that evening and night, so he spent the night at my house. The next day he met my kids, and I met his daughter Bailey, who was two. My parents were having a barbeque that day, so we went there, and he met my family. It seemed like a perfect match. I fell in love with his daughter, Bailey, and he said he fell in love with my kids. In less than four months after our first date, we were married and started our lives together.

I'm not going to say things were perfect because there isn't a perfect marriage. We both had exes and didn't have good relationships with them. We were a blended family, but the kids were close, and I felt we were as close to perfect as you could get. In July 1999, Devyn was born two months premature. We were in southern Missouri at the time and my mom and sister came to help with the other three kids so Ray and I could go to the hospital with Devyn. She was there for eleven days but she was strong and didn't have any issues after coming home. She wore an apnea monitor for six months, but it was just a precaution. We decided to move closer to my family in Northeast Missouri.

With four kids, we felt like life was complete. As the kids grew up, we kept them very active in sports, dance, gymnastics, church, 4-H, and other activities. We were always together, going on vacations and day trips. We had an array of animals and pets and spent a lot of time outside playing. My kids were everything and I loved planning crafts, holiday celebrations, devotions, and big birthday parties. I felt truly happy.

When Devyn was three or four, we decided to begin taking in foster children. We wanted to help kids and families. We were becoming more active in church and growing in our faith. Over the years we had many children come through our doors. Foster care was difficult, but I was hoping we were making a difference. There were challenges and sometimes I felt like dealing with the system was the most frustrating thing I had dealt with. We made our share of mistakes but tried to give every child that came through our house a chance at a different life. I loved every child that touched our doorstep, even though most of the time, I had no clue what I was doing. We had children who went back to their parents, other homes, or were adopted. It was always hard to see them go, but to this day, I still hope they know they were cared for.

In 2005, Michael and his older brother moved in with us and at that time he was eighteen months old. His older brother was a sweet kid but had a lot of behavioral issues that we didn't feel qualified to handle. Children's Division and the team felt like this might influence Mike's future behavior and they decided to move him to a different home. His older sister was in another home. The kids would have visits with each other and their biological parents, but it was sporadic. The foster care system has its share of flaws and it seemed to take forever before they terminated parental rights. These kids were in limbo for years. The parents would do enough to drag things out and then they would mess up again and we would be back to square one. I realized it was important to try reunification, but years of these children having no permanency was frustrating.

Thankfully, for Mike, he only knew and remembered our home. He remembered some of his visits, but it didn't seem to influence his thoughts and behaviors as much as it did his siblings. In 2013, when Mike was nine, parental rights were terminated, and we adopted him. After we left the courthouse, we had an adoption party for him, and he was all smiles. It was one of the best days for our family. My family felt complete.

At this time, Lily was married and expecting our first grandchild. The other kids were still at home in school. We stopped doing foster care several years before we adopted Michael because we wanted to focus on our kids. We fostered rescued pets for a while and the kids loved that. I had a few chewed-up seat belts and other destroyed household items, but it was a joy to help find forever homes for dogs and cats. Anyway, everything seemed perfect.

In 2014, we tore down an old barn beside our house and added on to the house. We turned our living room into a dining room and added a huge living room. The walls were made of tin and barn wood and the wall behind the television was made of wainscoting from the floor of the barn. It was gorgeous and I loved my house, and I was grateful that Ray had done most of the work himself, with help from our son-in-law. We had five bedrooms and three bathrooms. Downstairs we had a full basement with a pool table and ping-pong table and kids of all ages would hang out at our house. Life seemed to be moving along like we had planned, and I was very happy.

I thought Ray and I had this great relationship. He was very involved in the kid's activities and never missed anything they were in. He worked two jobs and when he was home, he helped with the house, grocery shopping, the kids, and took care of me. Friends would talk about how fortunate I was to have someone that was so helpful. He would surprise me with little things. I remember our first Christmas together. He bought me this beautiful necklace and hung it on our Christmas tree. It was there the whole time and I never saw it. He would do little things for me and always told me I was beautiful and that he loved me.

By 2015, three of our five children had graduated high school. Lily was married in 2012 and my first grandson was born in 2013. Josh was working, and Bailey was in college. Devyn had two more years of high school left. Ray and I were very active in our church. He was the vice-chair, and I was the secretary. Besides working, he loved to help the neighbors or anybody that asked. He also volunteered as vice-president of our school's athletic booster club. I thought Ray and I did everything together, even grocery shopping. I had no idea that I was married to a monster.

After Mike was adopted, it seemed his behavior changed over the next two years. He was not applying himself in school, and almost every night, Ray and he battled over his homework, especially math. I had a hard time handling Mike, and it seemed like he would listen better to Ray, so he handled more of his behaviors. I didn't realize until years later, that Ray was handling his behaviors with his belt, a little too hard. Mike didn't tell me this until a therapy session we had after everything came out.

Chapter 3: Back to July 8

Undeniable shock
Destroys from the inside,
Causes pain and anger,
Frustration and confusion.
Questions are left unanswered
And pieces of your heart die.

After hearing Mike's words, all I felt was numbness. I'm not sure how I got out of my chair and left work, but I remember getting in the car and telling Mike we would figure everything out and that I loved him more than he could know. I called my friend and pastor's wife, and then went to our church to speak to our pastor, Gary. Julie, his wife, showed up sometime during that time.

While Gary was talking to Mike, my mind immediately went back to a day a few years before when Josh told Lily that Ray had done something to him. I was coming home from one of the kid's sporting events when Lily called me and said she needed to talk to me. This was before she was married, and she was at Tony's mom's house. I pulled up to the front of the house and she came out and got in the car with me. She told me what Josh had told her, and I was shocked. She was shocked too.

I called Ray and asked him to meet me in town. We met and he got in my car. He looked confused and worried about what was wrong.

"I need to ask you something. Josh told Lily that you did some things to him."

He looked shocked and upset, but he wasn't angry. He said, "Honey, I would never do that. You know me. I have never hurt any of our kids. I love our kids."

I didn't know what to say or what to think. I couldn't imagine that Ray did something like this, but I was also confused about why Josh would say something like that.

I asked him to not come to the house until I had the chance to talk to Josh. He still denied doing anything to Josh inappropriate. I went home and spoke to Josh and he stated that Ray did bad things to him of a sexual nature. Looking back, I hate myself for that night because I just couldn't believe something like that could have happened and now wish I would have gone straight to the authorities. I asked Josh if he was sure and wanted to make sure he understood that

11

we would have to report it. Josh didn't want to talk about it but stuck to the fact that something had happened. I kept asking him if he was sure; I will never stop regretting questioning him. I wasn't angry with him but scared and confused. I knew that we would lose Michael since he was still a foster child. I knew that things would be different, even if Josh wasn't telling the truth. I asked Lily and Bailey if anything happened to them, and they said it didn't. I felt like Devyn and Mike were too young to ask.

I tried to call Ray but couldn't reach him. I was worried that something had happened to him. I went to Gary and Julie's house and talked to them. They were in shock and couldn't imagine Ray doing anything like that. Ray didn't come home that night and we tried to get some rest, but I couldn't shut my mind off. I knew we were going to have to take the next step in finding out what had happened. I was dreading turning my husband in to law authorities, but I knew we needed answers.

The next morning, Gary came over and talked to Josh. We gave them privacy and they talked about hunting and other interests that Josh had. Gary brought up Ray's name and Josh said that he made everything up because he was mad at Ray. I was in my bedroom, unaware of the content of the conversation when Josh knocked on my door. I came out and sat on the couch beside Josh and looked into his green eyes waiting for him to speak. Josh told me that he made the whole thing up and that he was so sorry. I was relieved but devastated that my beautiful son would make up something like that. He told me again how sorry he was, and I hugged him and forgave him, but I remember telling him that it would take time for me to trust him again. Those words still haunt me.

I was able to get a hold of Ray and he came home. I found out later that he had gone back to where he worked. He loaded barges at that time, and they had tall elevators and grain bins. He told me he had sat on top of one and contemplated jumping off.

The moment Ray walked in the door, Josh hugged him and told him how sorry he was for lying and that he loved him. The image of the two of them hugging and crying seemed so healing and touching that day, but now that image makes me sick. Josh wrote a letter to God apologizing for lying, but I found out later, he wasn't lying. At the time Josh wrote it, I thought he was taking responsibility for lying about Ray doing things to him. Now when I think about the content of that letter, anger is all I feel. It is hard knowing that Josh thought he had to hide what Ray did to keep the family together and happy.

Chapter 4

Sitting in the church, knowing what Michael had said and remembering that day with Josh, I knew I had to call Josh, who was now nineteen. I called all the kids and Josh was the first one to arrive at the church. He sat down by me and I could tell as I looked into his big green eyes that he knew something was wrong.

"Your brother has said some things about Dad, things that you said years ago. I need to know if what you said was true?"

Josh didn't even hesitate before telling me that it was true. I could tell that he was angry that Mike had been hurt. I was still in so much shock. I just wanted to think that maybe both the boys were mad at Dad and decided to say something about him. I know how that sounds, but that was the thoughts running through my mind. I couldn't imagine that this man that I had spent most of my adult life with was capable of this unimaginable thing. It didn't fit with who I knew. It didn't fit with the man who treated me like a queen. I was looking for any reason that the boys would say this.

I don't remember what order the three girls showed up, but Devyn and Bailey both denied that anything had ever happened to them. Lily was standing on the other side of the tables and Devyn was behind her against the wall near the kitchen of the fellowship hall. I remember Lily wrapping her arms around her waist and crying as she shook her head affirmatively that something had happened to her. The next thing I saw was Devyn sliding down the wall in tears and shock. Josh stood up quickly, pounded the church door open causing a loud echo as it hit the wall, and he stormed outside. I was there, but it was like I was watching a movie, a shocking story that couldn't be true. A story that my family couldn't be a part of. The pain, the anger, the overall shock had to be happening to someone else.

Trying to remember the exact order that things happened is difficult, but I remember enough to highlight the important things. At some point, while we were at the church, Gary called Ray and met with him. Ray now worked for the water district to be closer to home. He was out working somewhere. Gary met him where he was working and asked him about the accusations and Ray denied that anything happened. I remember Gary coming back to the church, but I don't remember how long it was or exactly how it happened, but somehow, we found out that Ray was talking about committing suicide. Gary called the sheriff's department, and we all went back to the house. They were trying to find Ray using his cell phone signal, but we lived in such a rural area that it was pinging him in locations he wasn't at. I remember Ray's boss coming to the house. I was inside looking out the window and I saw Lily collapse into his arms, and he just held her on the porch. It was painful to see how much hurt my children were going through.

There were so many people looking for Ray. At that time, law enforcement didn't know what was going on or what was happening. They just knew that he was threatening to kill himself and trying to find him. He called some of the kids on their cell phones and was talking ridiculous and not making any sense. He didn't call my phone during that time. At one point during the search, he sent Gary pictures on his cell phone of himself with some sort of rope, wire, or string around his neck. Gary called him and talked to him, and he finally said that he was behind our house near the ditch that ran down the field line. Josh grabbed our Gator and went with law enforcement to find Ray.

We all waited, terrified, of what they were going to find. Was he dead? Did he do something after he hung up with Gary? It was only a few minutes but seemed like an eternity passed. When the Gator pulled back in the driveway, I saw Ray in the back of it. He fell off the Gator when it stopped and seemed to have seizure activity and foaming at the mouth. At the time, I was terrified that he had taken pills and overdosed. They loaded him in the ambulance and asked Lily to ride with them because she was in EMT classes and almost finished with the classes. Unfortunately, due to Ray's behavior of thrashing around and kicking her in the ambulance, she never completed her testing to be an EMT. That is another thing he took from our family.

I am almost positive now that Ray was faking and didn't attempt to kill himself. He did have a line on his neck but that can be done without a lot of pressure. He had been talking to Gary on the phone to tell him where he was at and then after law enforcement found him, he suddenly was out of it and thrashing around. There was no kind of drugs in his system. He did have one of his rifles with him, but I think it was a ploy to distract from the real issue; the truth of his sexual abuse was coming out. But, at the time, I believed him, and it scared me that he tried to take his life.

Part of my journal entry from August 21, 2015:

I still couldn't believe that this man that I had spent seventeen years with this man who did so much for me was capable of being a monster. That was all put on hold when we couldn't find Ray and he was trying to kill himself. To be honest, I wonder if he really did try or if he was just trying to get attention or maybe make a distraction to not have to face the reality of what he did. Either way, it was a horrible day.

Chapter 5

After the ambulance left, Julie took me to the hospital. I called Ray's mom and sister and they came to the hospital from southern Missouri. Before I even saw Ray, I was talked to by a social worker who had already spoken with Lily. I had no idea what to believe at that time, but I remember telling her that I had a hard time believing Ray could do the horrible things he was accused of. I thought I knew him better than anyone.

When I finally got to see him in his hospital room, the first thing I noticed was it didn't seem to be the man I was married to lying in that bed. There was something different about his eyes. The blue of his eyes was dull, and he stared at me like he hated me. It scared me.

"Just leave me alone. You think I'm some kind of animal, so just let me be," he said.

"Ray, stop. Talk to me. I need to know what's going on."

"Just go. I can tell you think I'm some horrible person."

I leaned down and kissed him on the cheek and told him we would get to the bottom of everything. I still had the mindset that this wasn't possible. That was the last time I talked to Ray that evening. The next day, they transported him to a 96-hour hold in Columbia. He called me from there and it seemed like he was back to the Ray I thought I knew. I was at Lily's house and stepped outside to talk to him. He denied everything and told me things would be okay.

After his 96-hour hold, he was being discharged. Gary and Julie's son was a college student in the same town, and he picked up Ray and brought him back to our county. I met them in front of the newspaper office I worked at and took Ray to the house to get his clothes and his truck. I made sure none of the kids were at home. We were both crying while he was packing some of his stuff. He kept denying that he had done anything. When he left, he hugged me tight and told me, again, that everything was going to be okay and that our family would be back together soon. I wanted to believe him, but watching him drive away in his truck, I knew things would never be the same.

Chapter 6

On July 14, my birthday, and six days after Michael told me about the abuse, I had to take him to a child advocacy center so they could interview him. Gary and Julie drove us there and I was still holding on to a small glimmer of hope that nothing had happened. The people at the center were really nice and I was hoping Michael would feel comfortable enough to talk to them either way. They made us feel comfortable and the walls were painted in warm, friendly colors. I waited in a small waiting room with Gary and Julie while they interviewed Michael. In my mind, I was thinking they would talk to him, and find out that he was just mad at Dad and was making things up. I can't explain my mind because I was still in shock. I wasn't comprehending that two of my other children had said the same thing. All I could think is that there had to be an explanation that would make everything go away. The wait was excruciating long.

After Mike was interviewed, he came back to the waiting room. I couldn't tell anything by his expression. They then called me back and Mike stayed with Julie. Gary was with me for support and when I walked in the interview room, I noticed a DFS worker and deputy from our county along with three people from the advocacy center. Any hope I had of discovering Ray was innocent of what he was accused of was quickly dissipated by the looks of complete shock and anger that ran across the faces of everyone in that room. These people deal with sexual abuse issues every day and the looks on their faces left no room for doubt. I immediately started crying and was unable to comprehend anything that was being said to me. I was unable to listen and my mind was a nebulous mess. The caseworker from the Division of Children's Services said she would meet with me later and go over the findings with me. We left the center and took Mike to Taco Bell. I tried to be strong for Mike but inside I was falling apart. I wanted to cry, scream, and tear something up. It was an all-consuming anger that I had to swallow. It hurt going down, but I had to keep it at bay while I was sitting next to Mike.

Chapter 7

Michael went home with Gary and Julie, and I went back to my house. I was alone and my anger raged under the surface. I grabbed trash bags and started screaming and crying as I threw the rest of Ray's stuff into trash bags. I didn't care if I destroyed his stuff. I just wanted every part of him out of my house. I was in my bathroom that adjoined my bedroom and Devyn walked in during my rage. I knew that Devyn wanted to believe that her dad wasn't capable of hurting anyone. She had always been close to her dad. They raised huskies together for her FFA project and she was a daddy's girl. I don't think, until that moment, that she truly believed he was a monster. I could tell by her face that she, like me, realized that it really did happen. My heart shattered at the expression on her face and the tears in her blue eyes. It was only the beginning of her hurt. She might not have been a victim of sexual abuse but her and Bailey were both victims to the devastation of losing their father due to his behaviors. I knew it was only the beginning of how our lives were going to change.

September 14th Journal Entry

Devyn found out she was a homecoming candidate and cried so much when she realized that Ray won't be there for her and won't be walking her across the field. It made me so angry with Ray. If I would have seen him, I probably could have caused him physical pain. He text me and I said I didn't want to talk. He then sent seven messages, so I text him what was wrong. He then sent 12 messages and kept saying he was sorry, and he hates himself and why does he get to live. I didn't respond to any of them. Friday morning, I received two messages, so I called him and told him I was going to the Women's Retreat and didn't want 100 messages from him. He cried but respected my wishes.

Chapter 8

Ray kept trying to text and call me that day and I ignored him. He knew we were going to the advocacy center for Mike to be interviewed and I'm sure he realized that the results weren't what he wanted. The next day, deputies came to the house and collected evidence from the shed. They collected a marker and a trash can. I had to sign a paper that they took those items. I was standing in the kitchen cooking hamburger for tacos when the deputy came back in with the evidence list. I realized this was worse than I originally thought. Ray was arrested two days later and charged with two counts of statutory sodomy and taken to the county jail.

I felt embarrassed and ashamed. I didn't want to be around anyone or face anyone in our small community. I felt like they were asking themselves the same question I was asking myself: "How could I not know?" I still ask myself that every day and will never understand how the person you are the closest to can actually be a monster wearing a disguise of a good husband, father, Christian, and community member. I wanted answers and I wanted to be strong for my kids, but I felt weak and scared. I have continually replayed our lives together, looking for any clues I missed. It is hard to believe how easily I was deceived.

A couple of days later, the worker from children's services met with me at our church. Gary and Julie were with me. She told me some of the things that Mike had said during his interview. She read Josh and Lily's statements to me. It was too much. I didn't know how I was going to survive any of this. She recommended that our family find a counselor. I know it was a God moment because Gary knew of a counselor, and it was a perfect connection. He reached out to him and scheduled an appointment. Our church was gracious enough to pay for all our therapy and I don't think they can ever understand what an absolute blessing that was to me.

Chapter 9

I went to the first therapy appointment by myself. I wasn't sure I wanted this and wasn't sure I would feel comfortable talking to a strange guy about personal things. At this time, Scott had his office in his home. When I first saw him, all I thought of was the show Duck Dynasty. He was tall, skinny, and had curly gray/white hair that reached below his collar. I was terrified, but the moment he spoke, I felt better. I didn't sense any judgment from him. I didn't feel afraid of him. I felt like he was listening and sincere in his concern. I knew he was the right choice for our therapy.

Michael started to open up to me about the abuse. It was difficult to hear the details he shared with me. It made me sick, but I would listen and just hug him. He was very explicit in his descriptions of the abuse and it was sickening. The sad part was that what he told me was enough to make anyone sick, but he hadn't even scratched the surface of what happened to him and I wouldn't understand that until years later.

I wanted him to feel comfortable telling me anything he wanted so I remained strong during those discussions. It was behind closed doors and during therapy that I would break down. I spent a lot of time in the shower in tears.

August 22, 2015

As I was writing this entry, Michael just came in and told me stuff Ray made him do. It makes me sick to my stomach. It is hard for me to listen to that, but I know I need to be supportive of Michael and listen. So, earlier I felt guilty about not seeing Ray and now I feel like he should just rot in prison for the rest of his life. When will I ever get a grip on my emotions?

I wanted answers. I wanted to understand how this happened. I wanted to know the truth, no matter how much it hurt me. I went to the county jail and visited Ray. The sheriff's department and jail were in the bottom of the courthouse which was right across the street from where I worked. I also had questions about the house, or maybe that was my excuse. Ray had always taken care of maintenance things. I didn't even know how to change the furnace filter or anything remotely simple. He also took care of most of the bills and paperwork. I was not only facing the pain of what happened to my children, but I was dealing with going from two to one income, learning how to take care of things I had no idea about, and trying to juggle the emotions of each of my children. I was feeling overwhelmed.

Ray was not very nice to me the first time I visited him at the county jail and if it would have stayed that way, it would have been easier to cut ties. But it didn't. He later sent me a letter apologizing for how he acted. The next time I visited him I told him I needed to hear the truth from him, and I needed it now. He started crying and stated he did abuse the kids but that he didn't remember any of the abuse. He stated it was just starting to come back to him in dreams and so forth. I believed him and thought he had something wrong with his brain and that he didn't realize what he was doing.

Chapter 10

August 21st journal entry

Love, hate, guilt, loneliness, despair. God had been the only thing to get me through all of this. Today was another long day. The bond reduction hearing and new accusations. If I would have known Ray would have been gone a long time ago. I'm angry about so many things. At times, I am angry with God and question why he didn't bring this to light a long time ago? Why did this happen to my kids? Why did my family get torn apart? Why God? Why? WHY? WHY? WHY? I don't want to be alone. I don't want to be single. I don't want this pain. I don't want to face the uncertainties. I'm scared. I'm mad. I'm so mad! Two marriages and both failed. What is wrong with me? I'm angry with Ray. At times, I can't stand to see him. I have been visiting him, bringing him stuff and trying to be a friend by justifying that I'm showing God's grace and I believed that. But now I wonder. I wonder if I was holding on to him. I wonder if I'm scared to let go. Part of me wants to be in his arms again. But when I remember what he did I am disgusted with myself and hate myself. Could that be why I was okay with him making bond? Am I holding on? I want to forgive, and I want to have compassion for others, but maybe, I need to distance myself from him. I have been holding on to something not real and I have to let go.

August 22nd, 2015

I have visited Ray every Saturday, but I didn't tonight. I finally realized how much I am holding on to him and I am trying to let go. I had so much fun with my kids and watching Lane at the beach but when six o'clock rolled around, I felt guilt over not visiting him. I don't understand, but I guess a part of me feels bad knowing that no one visited him tonight and knowing that he was alone. But why, Lord, do I have to care? The horrible things he did is why he is in there. Lord, please help me be at peace with moving forward with the divorce.

Journal Entry August 25, 2015

Well, God, I'm falling apart. What do I do? Ray made bond today and talking to him has been so difficult, but I want to talk to him face to face. I want to yell at him and tell him all the pain he has caused our family. Then things keep falling apart at home. I'm thankful Gary fixed my water line Saturday and my breaker last night. Now, I find out that Michael is looking at sex videos online. Why is this happening? Lord, please protect my family. Please let me be at peace with the divorce. I'm going tomorrow to file. And my kids. I worry about them so much. The things he did to them are disgusting, sick, unreal, just unreal. I'm not strong today. I want to scream. I want to hit something, preferably Ray. Lord, I need you so much. Please help me. You know that I am struggling so bad and I don't know what I should feel or how I should act. I want to hate Ray, but I can't. Please Lord, please help me. You are an awesome God who has provided so much for my family, and I hate to ask for more, but I am desperate to feel your love and grace.

Ray's dad ended up posting bail and he was able to leave the county jail with an ankle bracelet on that would keep him within a ten-mile diameter of his dad's home. His dad lived about an hour and a half from our house in a very rural area. As crazy as it seems, I still craved answers. I made the drive to his dad's house to try and get answers. Ray was outside and when I stepped out of my car, I noticed how weak and broken he looked. We were standing in front of each other, and I started yelling at him and hitting him as hard as I could. He told me to keep hitting him because he deserved it and I did. I'm not sure how long it was before I almost collapsed. I was completely emotionally and physically exhausted. He was still claiming that he didn't have any memory of the abuse and he was so sorry for everything that he had done. I had cried and yelled so much that I barely had strength to think about the drive home, but I knew I needed to get away from this pain.

I was getting ready to leave and was leaning against my car. He touched me and I wanted to hate it, but I wanted to be comforted and Ray had always been my comforter. He had been my best friend for so many years, and he knew me better than anyone. He knew all of my insecurities and what I needed when upset. When he hugged me, it was like everything went away, and it was just him and I. It was almost like nothing had ever happened. When I left, I hated myself for letting him comfort me, for giving him that control over me. I cried the whole way home.

August 30.2015

So, Thursday, I went to see Ray at his dad's house. I was prepared for him to try and manipulate my feelings and try to keep me from divorcing him. But he didn't. Instead, he took full responsibility for everything and put all the blame on him without excuses. I yelled at him. I told him he disgusts me and what he did was sick. He told me to hit him and I did. I hit him a lot and I yelled, and he took every bit of it. He told me that I never let myself show my anger, but I really don't know how. He also told me that he will not fight me on anything and even though he doesn't want a divorce, he will give me everything. I told him how unworthy I feel and how he destroyed me. He told me how beautiful I am and how much he loves me, but I have a hard time believing him after what he did. He says he doesn't remember what he did to the boys and that he is praying that God shows him everything. When I got ready to leave, he hugged me, and it stirred up so many emotions. I told myself I would feel that way and that I wouldn't ever make love to him, but at that moment it was like everything went away and it was just me and him. I wonder if I would have given into how my body felt. That sickens me after what he did, but then again, I love him and that was a part of us for 17 years. I could tell that he wanted me in that way but as bad as he wanted me, he wouldn't do that to me because he knows that I would regret it later and he couldn't cause me any more pain, so we said our goodbyes. But I wonder if something is wrong with me since I have those sexual feelings for him. How can I be in love or want to make love to a monster, a pedophile, someone who did the worst possible evil to my kids. Lord, is something wrong with me? I feel so much guilt and shame. I'm still angry too.

September 6, 2015

I'm so confused. I miss being intimate with him, but I am disgusted by what he did. My therapist says these feelings are normal, but I still feel guilty.

Chapter 11: The new accusations

The days and months ran together after Ray was arrested and there was a lot that happened during that time. I would attend every one of Ray's court appearances and Gary went with me to all of them. Since Ray and I had been foster parents, letters were sent out to every child that had been in our home. I remember one child messaging Josh and stating that he couldn't believe Ray was accused of doing something so horrible. I don't think Josh ever wrote back that I know of.

Another child came forward and said that Ray did abuse him and that the whole family knew about it. I was at work when the DFS worker called me and asked if I could come across the street to talk to her. I asked if she could just come to my office, but she said that she preferred that I come there. The sheriff's department and interview rooms were in the basement of the courtroom. She took me into a concrete interview room and a deputy was also in the room. He instantly started reading me my rights. I was shocked, confused, and angry. They explained that it was standard during questioning. They explained the situation and the accusations made by this child stating that the other kids knew and that I knew that Ray was abusing him.

I made it very clear that if I would have known, I would have done something immediately. I reminded them that we were prepared to go to the law the day Michael told me, but everything got confusing with Ray missing and threatening to hurt himself. I wish I would have known. I wish I would have realized what he was capable of the first time he touched Lily, the first time he touched Josh, the first time he touched Mike. He would have been gone the minute I knew he had done that. I will continually carry guilt around about Josh telling us years before and not believing him. No amount of therapy will change that.

Nothing ever came out of the accusations, but it made me feel even worse. The child's story didn't make sense, but even though I knew that the kids or I didn't know anything about what was said, a part of me wondered if Ray didn't hurt this child. It was a mixture of emotion; anger for being accused of something so untrue, and pain of wondering how many children Ray did hurt. I will always wonder if there were other children who suffered because of him. It makes me sick to think that there might be kids out there who are still living with the pain and embarrassment of what he did to them.

I tried to get answers out of Ray so I could understand, but I quickly realized that no matter what he said, nothing could make anyone understand what he did. In March 2015, I wrote a novel. I loved to write and penned the book in three months. The book was about a teenager that was in the foster care system and had been sexually abused by a foster parent. Ray stayed up all night and read my book. This was a few months before I found out what he did. I later asked him how he read my book and still continued to do what he did. He told me that he wrote me a letter confessing everything and was going to give it to me but ended up burning it. He said there had been several times he wanted to come clean over the years, but if that was true, why didn't he stop the abuse. I now realize it was another lie he told me.

Chapter 12

The kids continued to struggle with so many emotions and changes. Our income situation was different. Their dad was gone. Struggles were everywhere, but they were so brave. There were times where their emotions and anger were too much for them. I understood. I was right there with them.

Journal Entry September 27, 2015

Last Sunday Josh couldn't get the oil filter off his car and he felt worthless and incompetent. He got mad and hit the fridge, throwing and breaking magnets and the broom. It scared me. He later said it scared him and that he has a lot of anger in him. He is really angry with Ray but at times he cries because he misses him. Michael struggles with the same emotions. I took him to the doctor this week and he is started on medicine to help him focus. I hate putting kids on medicine, but he is struggling in school and hopefully this will help. Thursday was the pep rally and I had to go take pictures. When the senior dads were out there with the senior boys, I realized that Michael would be a senior someday and he won't have a dad there. That made me very angry with Ray. I told him how I felt, and he cried and did his self-pity thing that makes me mad. I was so angry with him but don't want him to hurt himself or do something stupid.

*Friday was hard too. Ralph and Amanda (*friends from church*) helped with the parade and Ralph's friend drove Devyn in his jeep for the parade. Ralph brought her a rose. That evening, I walked her out across the field. She only wanted my name mentioned. She is hurt and ashamed by what her dad did. I felt like everyone was looking at us even though they might not have been. It was a very difficult evening.*

Lily let Lane talk to him on the phone for Lane's sake. She wants to take Lane to see him and say goodbye. It was hard on Lily because she is really angry with Ray but misses him too. Devyn said she doesn't want to see him because she feels it will make it harder on her. Josh and Michael want to see him but can't because of the investigation. Bailey doesn't open up much about things. I miss her being here.

Chapter 13

During the time that Ray was in jail, I did visit him. Every time he would find a way to make me feel bad for him. He started talking about having dreams and memories of his dad abusing him. He talked about remembering a big bed where the abuse from his father took place. He talked about his childhood and that he didn't remember much. He said his family was filling in some forgotten memories. When our kids were little, Ray had told me that his dad had sexually abused his sister, and that he never wanted our kids to be alone with his dad. He had denied that anything had happened to him or his brother. I now realize the one they needed protected from was him.

Journal Entry September 27, 2015

Saturday, I went to see him at his dad's house after Michael's game. We talked a lot and I read all of the investigation stuff from his lawyer. It sickens me to think about what he did. I will never understand how he can hurt our children that way and how he looked in the mirror each day. I believe he really doesn't remember what he did. He remembered Lily's abuse but not the boys. As he has prayed, he is remembering, and the statements confirm a lot of his memories. He told me about his childhood and what his family has told him. He doesn't remember any of it: trying to kill his mom twice, pulling a gun on his brother, the four-wheeler accident and head injury, the time in a mental institution and much more. It doesn't excuse his behavior but shows how much he needs help. He is ready to confess and take whatever the judge sentences him to. I'm glad but also confused because he is facing more than one life sentence and I don't know if he should go away that long. He thinks he can help other people. He needs help, a good therapist and he wants that too. But I also realize that I can't worry or try to control the situation and I need to turn it over to God.

He said he was starting to have dreams of what he had done to the kids and he realized he wasn't himself during that time. He would talk about how much he missed me, his kids, and grandson. It was all about how hard this was on him. He would tell me the things he had heard about child molesters in prison and that he could lose his life. He would claim that God had changed him, and he could help other people who have done these things if he wasn't in prison. I wish I could say that I didn't feel sorry for him, that I didn't buy into everything he said. He knew how to make me feel sorry for him. He knew my heart, he knew my compassion, he knew my love, and he exploited them for his benefit.

When Ray was in the county jail, he asked for pictures of the family. I took him some and didn't give it any thought. A few days later, I received a call from the caseworker at children's services, and she asked me why I would give him pictures. I didn't see what the big deal was. She basically made it clear that a lot of pedophiles will use the pictures to masturbate to. I thought that was ridiculous and made it clear that I didn't see him being the type to do that. I was still caught in this limbo of not being able to reconcile the Ray I had known with the evil Ray. To me, they were two different people.

I continued to visit Ray at his dad's house. More than anything, I wanted answers and as hard as it is to admit, I still cared for him, and didn't know how to live my life without him in it. I couldn't understand how he could have done these horrible things. How does anyone look at a child that way? I wanted answers and I needed answers. It didn't matter what he said. Nothing made sense. There was no excuse for the things he did.

Journal Entry September 6, 2015

Ray also claims to not remember what he did to the boys and when he asked questions that I couldn't answer, he realized that he had done horrible things. He literally became sick and began vomiting. He is either a really good actor or telling the truth. How do I know? Lord, help me discern.

My kids confuse me too. Josh and Michael were victims of horrible abuse and they hated it and him, but yet they love him too. Michael wanted me to take him licorice yesterday and tell him that he loves him. Yet some days he hates him.

Ray continued to claim that he didn't remember what he had done, and it continued to come back to him gradually. One day, we were sitting in his bedroom at his dad's house. I told him some of the things Michael had told me but couldn't bring myself to answer all of his questions. Ray acted shocked. He cried and went as far as going in the bathroom to vomit. He seemed so upset and sickened by what he did. In that moment I felt bad for him. I honestly wondered if he had something wrong where he didn't remember doing these things, almost like he was another person when he abused the kids. I wanted to believe that the man I was married to for so many years was the man I thought he was. I didn't want to accept that he was capable of these things. He constantly put thoughts in my mind, and I wanted to believe they were true. I had no idea how manipulative he could be, and how easily I could fall into that manipulation. I always thought people were crazy who had been manipulated. How could they believe that? How could they fall for it? Well, let me tell you, it happens. It happens to people who never thought they were capable of being manipulated.

Chapter 14

Ray was arrested again at the end of September on new charges. He called me at nine-thirty p.m. that evening and told me they were arresting him on new charges from 2005. I had been used to talking to him every day and even though I knew I shouldn't be emotional about him being arrested, I was. I was still frustrated that it wasn't revealed years ago and that we didn't listen to Josh when he said Ray did something to him. Gary and I went to his dad's house and picked up his truck. It was hard to have it in my driveway again and Lane knew it was "Papa's truck" which made it hard. We didn't know how to explain things to Lane. He was around eighteen months old when Ray was arrested and was going to turn two in November. He still remembered him.

I was still struggling with my conflicting emotions and had no idea how to process them. I was glad to have my therapy with Scott. I felt comfortable being honest and real with him.

Journal entry October 5, 2015

I was telling Scott about the guilt I felt for loving Ray. He said God welded us together for 17 years and it isn't easy to turn off love. He said I should allow myself to love him so I can grieve my loss. I do love him, but it hurts so bad. My kids love him too. Loving him doesn't mean I condone what he did. It disgusts me when I think about what he did to my children.

With all my struggling emotions, my first and most important priority was my kids. But I made my share of mistakes. I had a lot of stress on me financially, spiritually, and emotionally. I struggled to make ends meet with one income. When Ray was out of prison, he tried to help some, but it wasn't the same as when we were married, and both worked. I wanted to control everything and make things perfect for my kids, but I was floundering on my own. I had a wonderful church family that I am thankful for, but we all had this anger building up inside of us.

Journal Entry October 15, 2015

Well, this week went to crap pretty quickly. I tried to talk to Josh Sunday and he had an angry outburst. It scares me and upsets me to see so much anger in him. Then Monday was a really bad day. I was still feeling bad about asking Ray for space and then I felt bad because he was actually giving it to me. When we got home, Michael was having a really bad attitude and I was trying to cook supper. He wanted me to help him right then and I couldn't because I was cooking supper. He started saying mean things and hurtful things. I asked him to be quiet and work on his math. He later threw another fit and wouldn't do his math. When I grabbed him out of the chair, he resisted, and I pulled ligaments in my left arm.

I was also mad because he and Devyn didn't do any chores after school. At supper, I said something to Devyn, and she said I didn't tell them to do the dishwasher. They are 16 and 11!!! I just lost it. I threw my plate and yelled, grabbed my keys, and left the house. I don't know where all that anger came from. I had already, thirty minutes earlier, went to the lake and cried out to God, but when I got home, I still lost it. Devyn said I looked at her and told her I was sick of her. That breaks my heart. I meant that I was sick of everything. How am I supposed to be mom and dad? I am failing miserably! I'm so mad at myself.

The next day, Devyn and Josh said they felt like they lost their dad and was losing their mom too. I feel awful! My kids are everything to me and I don't want to ever hurt them. Devyn also said she thought she had the perfect dad, but she didn't. She said she doesn't want anybody to know that he is her dad. That what he did disgusts her, and she can't claim him. But she says she is fine. She is not fine.

Journal Entry October 21, 2015

I went to visit Ray today. We only had 10 minutes. Our divorce has been moved up to next week and I wanted to talk to him about that. I left the visit mad and I am still really ticked off at him. He seemed upset that I was getting everything and said he doesn't trust my lawyer. Then he kept joking with me and the prisoner next to him. He even tried to lean over into their picture while I was talking to him. Our time was short, and he couldn't give me the respect to focus on our conversation for ten minutes. I went back to work and typed him a letter. I don't have to visit him. I don't have to bring him candy.

Journal Entry October 24, 2015

Today was a good day, a really good day. We had a very emotional therapy session last night and Josh is really struggling because he is missing Ray and it made me realize the house can feel empty without Ray. Josh and him always picked on me at suppertime when I was cooking. Last night Josh said things will never be normal because Ray will never walk in the *door again. The reason he didn't tell is because he didn't want the family to fall apart. It breaks my heart that he took all that on himself all those years. But today was better. Josh set up the deer stands with a friend. And went hunting. Bailey was home and Lily and Lane were here. I had all five kids and my grandson here. Laughter, joking, licorice flying across the kitchen. Just a nice day. Then I kept Lane while Tony and Lily went to a wedding. Lord, thank you for a good day.*

Chapter 15

I tried to keep things as normal as possible for the kids. In October 2015, we had a big Halloween party at the house. During the party, the sewer backed up and the basement carpet was wet, so we had thirty-five kids upstairs watching "Poltergeist." After several calls, I finally was able to talk to Ray at the jail about the sewer since I knew nothing about it. Over the next couple of days, the men from church worked on it and was able to get it unclogged. We had to replace the carpet downstairs. It was frustrating that even when we were trying to keep things normal, move on, enjoy life, I still felt like I had to reach out to him when something went wrong.

My divorce from Ray was finalized in October. I was confused about how I should feel about that. Ray kept telling me that our marriage would be restored and that we would become a cord of three with Jesus in the middle. I wanted him to quit saying things like that because my emotions were already a mess. I knew without a doubt that I didn't want to be married to him anymore, but I also felt lost. He kept saying, "God brought us together, and he will restore our family." I would tell him that I didn't get any of those feelings when I prayed. He kept trying to convince me that I needed to keep praying because he knew that is what God wanted. I felt like I was failing in my prayer life since Ray was so adamant that this is what God wanted. What was wrong with me that I wasn't getting those answers or feelings when I prayed to God? Nothing in my prayer life made me feel like God would restore what we had, but Ray kept convincing me that He would.

The kids were so confused too. Josh had decided he wanted to join the Army. I thought it would be good for him, but he ended up changing his mind.

Journal Entry November 15, 2015

Josh decided not to join the army. He said he doesn't have the motivation to exercise. He only works and not much else. I worry so much about him. The other evening Lily and he got into a big argument about Josh taking out the trash and he just went off yelling and cussing and I don't know how to handle it. He is hunting today and doesn't do much else.

Ray got out of jail and went to his dad's house with the ankle bracelet. I visited him a couple of times over the holidays. I wanted to completely let go, but I was still unable to do that. The kids still struggled with so many emotions. Bailey was in college, and I didn't hear from her as much as I wanted to. I knew each of the kids had different ways of coping with their grief, so I gave her space. Devyn had no desire to talk to him or say goodbye to him. Lily struggled and wavered back and forth about talking to him and if she should. Michael was still struggling with behavioral issues. Josh was my biggest concern. He struggled with anger and refused to pick up after himself.

In January 2016, my pastor, Gary, and two other men from our church went to visit Ray at his dad's house. I wasn't there for their conversation, but Gary later told me that they were straightforward with him and told him that if he truly wanted God's forgiveness, he needed to be honest. Unlike me, they knew that he was aware of exactly what he had done. Ray finally admitted that he did remember everything that he did. So, once again, all the acting like he didn't remember, the tears, the pretend vomiting, and more was all fake. At that time, I still didn't see it because he was constantly in my ear; constantly telling me a different story.

Chapter 16

Gary and I continued to go to all the court appearances. On February 11, 2016, Ray confessed on the stand. I was so happy that the kids wouldn't have to go through a trial, but I was terrified of losing him. I had been single for over half a year, but I still struggled on how to function in that role. When Ray confessed on the stand, the judge stated that he had never had a defendant in the courtroom like Ray that had taken so much responsibility for his actions. At the time I was thinking, "See, even the judge sees that Ray is different than other people that do this." The truth was that Ray was that good at manipulation. He had a way of making people not look at what he did.

The judge approved family therapy sessions with Scott. Ray and I had already met with Scott, and we hoped this would help the kids heal. Scott had told me that it really depends on Ray to know how the sessions would go. We had our first family session in February. We had two Saturday sessions and Josh and Michael had sessions with Ray.

During Michael's session, Ray said, "I'm so proud of you for telling what happened. I'm really proud of you."

"I'm proud of you, Dad, for telling the truth," said Mike.

Ray took responsibility for what he did and apologized to the whole family.

Everyone, except Devyn, hugged Ray after the sessions, and I was happy that it went so well. Scott had prepared me that sometimes the perpetrators don't always take responsibility, so I felt like this was a big step in the healing process for the kids. Looking back, I do think it was helpful as part of the healing process, but I do believe this was another tactic of Ray's to stay part of the family. He knew what to say and how to be a good person. He had fooled me and others for many years and I believe he continued to do that during the therapy.

Journal Entry February 23, 2015

Ray was so open and real and made no excuses. He took all responsibility. He told Mike how proud he was of him. He told Josh how proud he was of him for going to therapy and talking to Scott. Josh yelled at him. Devyn wouldn't look at him or even acknowledge him. The kids shared good memories and values Ray has taught them. They told him they hate him but love him too. Josh said he didn't care what happened to him. He just hated to see his family hurt. Scott talked about how different our family was and used the word resilient. He talked about how the kids still love Ray. I am glad that Ray is how he is now but wish he would have been this man before. I know we can't change the past. It is just so hard. He told the kids about how he lied to me because he did know that he hurt the boys. He had just blocked out details because he didn't want to talk about it. He told me on Friday he wanted to be like clear glass to me and be completely honest, but it is hard to hear some of what he says.

March 6, 2016

A lot has happened in the last few weeks. We had our second family session and even Devyn participated a little bit. It went better than I could have anticipated. Ray had individual sessions with Josh and Michael. Michael wanted me with him for his session. He opened up a lot. I hope Michael's behavior improves with knowing that none of it is his fault and Ray takes full responsibility. I spoke to the probation officer for the sentencing report, and he also spoke to Josh. Josh later told me that he told the guy he thought it was stupid to go away for 22 years. Ray wants Lily and I to make statements at his sentencing on Thursday. Yesterday, I went and saw Ray. He said he has completely surrendered his life to God and is at peace with the 22 years and even at peace with death. He told me about his board and nails and how he finally burned it and surrendered his life and everything to God. It was so hard to leave him yesterday.

The sentencing hearing was scheduled, and Ray was still constantly in my ear. He convinced me to vouch for him, convinced me that he could do so much more if he weren't in prison, convinced me that he could help others, and help stop this happening to other kids. I wish I could explain manipulation, but there is no way to understand it, even if you realize later how manipulated you were.

When I was with him, it was like the rest of the world didn't exist. We would go eat or watch a movie at his dad's. We spent time outside and talking. I was still in the denial stage of accepting what really happened. My mind knew, but my heart was having a hard time catching up.

Chapter 17

During the sentencing, Lily and I read letters that we had written. I regret my letter now. I was very clear that I could never excuse what Ray had done, but I highlighted all the things that I thought were good about Ray. I spoke with the prosecutor and tried to convince him that Ray would be better off going somewhere where he could help people that might want to hurt kids. He could share his story and mistakes. I remember him asking me if this was fair to the kids, if this is what they wanted. I knew, at that time, it was what they wanted, because, like their mother, they didn't believe he was a monster. That doesn't mean that it was the right answer.

I later realized that everything I said to the lawyer were words from Ray. Ray had me convinced that if he went to jail, he would be killed. He had talked to me a lot about how he could minister to others if he didn't go to jail and that he could prevent other kids from getting hurt. I continued to fall for everything Ray said. In March 2016, Ray was sentenced to seventeen years for two counts of statutory sodomy. It should have been a lot longer. I still blame myself for that. But, on that day, I was devastated that he would be gone for so many years. He was going to be transferred to Fulton that day. Lily and I went downstairs with him to the sheriff's office and told him goodbye. There were a lot of tears and a lot of fears of what I would do on my own. I can only imagine what the deputies thought watching me hug him and basically defend his character. I don't like the person I was at that time.

I hated the Ray that did the horrible things to my kids. I hated Ray on those days when Mike would tell me the unbelievable details of the abuse that Ray subjected him to. I never imagined anyone was capable of those things. Josh didn't talk much about the abuse, but I remember him telling me, "Mom, it is worse than you can ever imagine." Yet Ray would get in my head and make me think he wasn't like other sexual predators. I could see that the kids still loved their dad. Even the kids that were victimized remembered all the good "dad" things that he had done. They struggled like I struggled. Josh didn't want anyone talking bad about his dad even though he hated him for what he had done to him and his siblings. We were all conflicted and Ray was the master of manipulators. A manipulator that doesn't even realize how good he was at it.

But, even through that hate I felt for him, I truly believed that he was a different person. I believed he had changed. I defended him to other people and even spoke in church. I put a post he had written on Facebook. I never made excuses for what he did, but I realize now that defending anything about him was completely wrong. I was listening to him. I was missing him, and I was doing what he wanted.

Journal entry March 13, 2016

Today at church, I shared what God has done in Ray's life. It was very painful and difficult, but I wanted God to have the glory. I also read his post he wanted to put on Facebook. He didn't post it because of my worries and fears. Today, I shared on Facebook some of my feelings and Ray's thoughts. I'm scared of the reactions, but so far, they have been positive. As much as I hate speaking in front of people, I'm glad that I did. I wish I knew what all God wanted me to do but I know I will be sharing this story more in the future. God, please show me the path you want me to take. Don't let me focus on Ray or men in general, but on you. I need to draw close to you and have an intimate relationship with you. I can't do any of this on my own. I'm scared of the future, and I do worry, and I am asking for you to give me peace and to send your Holy Spirit to guide me.

I worried about everything. I was so afraid something else would go wrong or someone in my family would get hurt.

Journal entry March 31, 2016

Lord, as you know, my panic and anxiety has worsened. Every time someone says I need to talk to you or when something is wrong, I begin to panic and worry and think the worse. It was helpful talking to Scott today and it helped learning ways to deal with that. I am going to a movie and dinner with some friends. I can't believe I panicked when she asked for my personal email because I thought something was wrong.

The above journal entry was after I received a message from someone I knew. We weren't close friends, or someone I talked to a lot, but we were friendly since it was a small community. She sent me a message asking for my email and I thought something was wrong with one of my kids since she worked at the school. I felt ridiculous when I found out she wanted to invite me to dinner and a movie with friends. I caused myself a lot of anxiety over the whole situation.

Chapter 18

When Ray was first arrested, a restraining order was put against him for Devyn and Michael since they were both minors. After Ray went to Fulton, I was receiving letters and phone calls from him, and he kept talking about wanting to write the kids, but he wasn't sure if he could because of the restraining order. I struggled with what to do, but once again I listened to him. When I walked in the courthouse, I stared at the brown banisters and stairs leading upstairs and questioned myself about whether I should do this. I took the initial step and went the rest of the way up. I was ready to sign the paper reversing the restraining order, but the judge wanted to speak to me. He was friendly but had that look of scrutiny, the look people give when listening to someone defend a monster.

Journal Entry April 18. 2016

I went last week to end the order of protection for Mike and Devyn and had to sign a paper. I thought that was it but then the judge wanted to talk to me, and he signed it but wanted to make sure I understand what I am doing. How do I make people understand that Ray has changed?

I really believed that Ray had changed and that he was different. I had told myself and him that I forgave him. I didn't forgive him for his sake; I forgave him for my sake and because I knew that is what God would want. I am not sure if I ever truly forgave him though. I still hold on to so much anger about what he did and what continued to happen in our family. I believe with all my heart that God can change anyone but I also know that person has to surrender everything to Him. Ray said he did, but I still don't think he truly has. I think he still thinks he is different than most people who sexually abuse children. He continually made everything about his suffering and not the family's suffering.

Chapter 19

I visited Ray in Fulton. It was an extreme eye-opener. I had never been to a prison before. The whole process made me feel like a criminal. It was an experience that I don't want again. We visited with glass between us using phones. Of course, everything was about him and how rough he had it.

Ray would write me letters and I would write him letters. He would write to the kids. His letters would be all about his relationship with God and how God was going to use him in prison. He always was sure to tell me that God would bring us back together in the future. I still didn't feel any of that when I would pray but Ray was so convincing. Later Ray was moved to a maximum-security prison in southern Missouri. I visited him there and it was the same feeling I had when visiting him in Fulton. The difference was that we were able to sit at a table together in a big room and talk. We continued to write to each other, and he would call. I would help put money, money I didn't have, on his books so he could call and buy stamps. I would send song lyrics from some of my favorite songs. One time Mike wrote the lyrics to Ray's favorite Christmas song, "Little Drummer Boy." When I visited him in prison, we had our picture taken together. I later looked at that picture, with him in the gray jumpsuit, holding my hand, and wanted to be sick.

I remember waiting in line to visit him and hear people talking about the inmates they were visiting. I would hope and pray that no one would ask me questions. When I was in the room with him, there were tables throughout with people visiting. I knew the other inmates knew what he had done. It made me question myself and wonder what they thought of some woman visiting someone like him. He told me people would call him "Chomo" which is slang for child molester in prison. He said he wanted to stay in general population and face what he did. I have no idea if he is still in general population or in another part of the prison. But, when he told me that, it made me continue to think he was taking responsibility for what he did, and not hiding from it. I'm sure he has good behavior and prison because he is the master at being good.

Chapter 20

During those months, I grew closer to God. I craved a relationship and thankfully I held on to Jesus. I drowned myself in the Word and prayer. I led a Bible Study on the book of Leviticus at church and how the book was still relevant today. I wanted God more than anything. But I also continued to struggle with loneliness. I had my children and grandson who were everything to me. I had my friends who picked me up several times. But at the end of the day, I felt alone.

Journal Entry May 21, 2016

I haven't written in here for almost a month but that is because I haven't been good and I'm trying to avoid the pain. Lily walked in on me crying and I hate that because I have to be strong. I don't want the kids seeing me crying because I miss him. I hate that I miss him. I hate that I miss being married. I miss having a husband and someone to wake up to. Lord, I feel like I'm lost and barely treading water. I have no money. I'm stressed at work and I'm not keeping things in balance. Plus, I want my kids to be open and honest with me, but I know they don't want to hurt me. Lily finally told me about her memories and how some days she misses Ray and some days she doesn't want me or anyone talking to him. I understand and want my kids to be okay, but I can't even figure out my own emotions.

I have to figure out how to cope, grieve, truly grieve and move from the rut I am in. But, knowing that and doing that are two different things.

Chapter 21

Christmas 2016, I changed our tree topper and some of our Christmas traditions. Josh was very upset with me. He didn't want anything to change. He wanted our traditions and family things to stay the same. It was hard because I wanted things to change. I wanted rid of the past and rid of Ray even though we were still communicating. I still had a hard time talking about him in a negative way. I was trying to hold on to the Ray I thought I was married to. I couldn't except that the Ray I had known was fake and part of his manipulation was pretending to be a good person while he had been hurting my children over the years.

In December 2016, I had dived into the dangerous world of Facebook and online dating. I was still carrying so much guilt that I cared for Ray, still mad at myself for the time I spent with him, the times we went out to eat, the nights I slept at his dad's house. I was lonely. I felt used. I needed some type of reassurance that I was still desirable by someone that wasn't a monster. I started talking to a guy on a Missouri singles site on Facebook. We would message a lot and when he told me his age, I refused to date him. He was quite a bit younger than me and I didn't want to deal with that. But he was persistent, and he made me feel good. I was struggling with so many personal insecurities that I needed the positive validation.

The final weekend of December, Josh wanted to go with me to visit Ray. We were going to stay the night in a hotel nearby and the guy I was talking to on Facebook was going to meet us there. Josh and I went to the prison and visited Ray and it was a visit where they allowed food, so I made some of Ray's favorite things and we took them. Of course, Ray had many tears and said the same things he always did. Josh was with me and that gave me the courage to tell Ray I was going to start dating. He was not happy about it.

When Josh and I got to the hotel room, the guy called me and stated that he couldn't make it because something was wrong with his vehicle. Ray was in prison in Charleston, Missouri, and this guy lived across the state. The next day Josh and I drove to the other side of the state and met this guy and his dad at the Bass Pro Shops in Springfield. Josh and he hit it off, talking about hunting and fishing. We went for a walk without Josh and he informed me that he didn't have any money to take Josh and me out to lunch like planned. I gave him money for lunch because I knew Josh would be upset if I bought this guy's lunch and I needed Josh to like him. I was trying to make everyone happy while searching for something to make me feel better about myself.

After we ate lunch with this guy, Josh and I loaded up to make the long drive back home. My son had turned twenty-one in July, so getting him to open up about personal things was difficult. He talked a lot about his relationship with his ex-girlfriend, how much he loved her, and how much he missed her. We talked about Ray, and he still wouldn't talk about him in a negative way. I cherished every moment I had with Josh on this weekend trip. We laughed and joked but also had moments where we shared our hearts and struggles.

We arrived home shortly before midnight on New Year's Eve. When we got home, Devyn and her boyfriend had out the light sabers and playing with them on the stairs. It made me smile to see two high school kids having fun in a childlike fashion. It made the end of a great weekend even better.

Shortly after that, the guy we had met in Springfield called me and stated he had been kicked out of his house and that his dad was crazy. He convinced me to drive to Branson and pick him up. I explained that money was tight and that I wasn't ready to have a relationship full time or live with anyone. He promised he would only stay with me a few days while he figured out what he was going to do. He stayed in the basement and wouldn't leave. He tried to get a job but lasted one day before getting fired. He drove my mom around running errands and hung out with Josh. During his time there, I discovered that he lied about his age and was fifteen years younger than me. He drove my car and my mom's car all the time before I discovered that he didn't have a driver's license. I realized I was prone to find the best manipulators.

At first Josh and he got along great, but soon Josh felt like he was taking advantage of me. He told me I had to get rid of him or he would. Josh was very angry that he was still there. I was sitting at the end of my big farmhouse table in the dining room. Ray had made it from some of the barn wood we had left after adding on to the house. I had my laptop open and working on homework. I had decided last year to go back to school and get my degree in English and creative writing since I loved to write.

Josh was over six feet tall and stood by the table in red athletic shorts, an Oklahoma University t-shirt with the sleeves cut out and his personalized OU cowboy boots I had bought him for Christmas. I knew he was angry. He informed me that the guy had to go. I wanted the guy to leave too, but didn't know how to go about it. I tried to get the guy to leave on his own, but he wouldn't. I knew if I didn't do something soon, Josh was going to end up doing something we would all regret. I ended up taking this guy to a homeless shelter in Springfield. It was hard to leave someone there, but an absolute relief to be free of him.

Chapter 22

The twisted thorns of sin dig at my skin
The vines wrap tightly around me
Squeezing away the light.
The light has been darkened
And the pain is unbearable.
I keep embracing the darkness
But it is dangerous.
It is all-consuming.
It keeps the grief at bay
But only temporarily.

One thing I struggled with was feeling like something was wrong with me sexually. Men usually aren't criticized for saying they enjoyed sex. Women are. I enjoyed sex and I had always thought Ray and I had a healthy and good sex life. I couldn't understand how someone who had an active sex life with their spouse could hurt children in a sexual way. Scott explained how what Ray and I had was completely different than what he did to the kids. It wasn't a reflection on me, but even hearing that didn't help me. I wanted to feel desired and sexual.

I decided to try a different approach and joined some online dating sites. The next date I went on was with a guy who had a job and a lot of money. It seemed like the perfect date and a night of sex. I'm not even sure I enjoyed the sex. I was numb and felt this was the only way to heal. He took me home the next morning and I didn't hear from him again. I sent him one of those ridiculous text messages of how he used me and more. Then I sent him a text message trying to take that one back. I had no clue how to maneuver the dating life in my forties. Ray and I had been married so many years.

I continued to talk to guys. I did things I'm not proud of. I sent inappropriate pictures and text messages and received the same type of pictures from guys. I was used and used others. I kept thinking sex would make me feel better and numb the pain, but it didn't do any of that. I discussed it with Scott, and I thought I was done with dating. But I couldn't stop. I would talk to several guys at one time and I would have sex with some of them. I didn't care about myself and

I didn't respect myself. I went to bed at night hating myself but woke up living this life that wasn't me. I felt myself trying to hold on to God, but I was living this life of sin.

I had many guys that I started talking to online tell me these unbelievable stories trying to get money. One guy told me his mom had been in a wreck and he needed money to go see her on her deathbed. I had one who said he was in the military and he needed money sent to his kids for their birthdays because he was overseas and had no way to get money to them. I never gave any of them money. I knew some of the guys I talked to were dangerous.

There was one that I talked to for several months and he even created a Facebook page. I know now that everything was fake, but he was so good at convincing me that he was this great guy. When I started talking to this guy, I made it clear that I wouldn't give him money. He stated he didn't want that but that he just wanted me. He said he was a geologist working in another country and we would meet when he came home. Pictures he would send me were of a pale guy with red hair. When he would call me, he would have a strong Mexican accent. I questioned him about it, and he said he looked like his dad and that his mom was from Mexico. We talked about marriage and love and more. I knew he wasn't the person he said, but it was like living in some kind of fantasy world. It was like reading a good book; it took me away from the "real world." He even had his "daughter" correspond with me through email. Several months later, he started asking me for money for his daughter's illness. He was very convincing, but I never gave him money. He became very angry and even threatened me. I blocked him and never spoke to him again.

Online dating was a very different world and I got wrapped up in it in the worst possible way. But, with all I was doing in my little bit of free time, my time was mainly spent with my kids. I needed them and they needed me. Devyn had her junior and senior year to go through with a single mom and a lot less money. She was so strong through all those changes. Bailey was at college, succeeding, but having her own personal struggles. Josh was working and in March 2017, he and his best friend got their own place. I knew how hard he struggled with guilt. He felt like he should have stuck to his story years ago or told what happened and it might not have happened to Mike. No matter how often we told him he was a victim and not responsible, he still carried guilt. Lily, her husband, and my grandson would come over a lot for supper. I knew Lily struggled with a hole in her heart from not having a dad. Both of her dads had failed her, and it broke my heart that all she wanted was a normal relationship with a father and the two she had

had failed her. Mike struggled with anger and his behaviors only escalated. The kids were and always will be my world. I tried to spend quality time with him, going on our own little date nights, go for walks, or take a ride in our Mule.

Chapter 23

Ray continued to write letters and I was getting to the point where I didn't read them. They were usually twelve pages long, so twenty-four front and back, and it was the same thing over and over. I started to realize how much he was about himself even though he tried to make it look like he cared for others. I started to see him for who he was, but I didn't know how to break that bond. I kept answering his calls and I started to realize how much control he had over me.

He would talk about some of the guys he was in prison with and he had made friends with another guy that was in prison for sexually abusing children. He was from our area. Ray kept drilling in my head how I needed to reach out to this guy's wife and talk to her about how I still talked to him and forgave him. I would refuse and put it off, but he wouldn't stop pressuring me. He even asked me to write this guy letters. He wouldn't let it go and I didn't have the strength to keep fighting him. I finally gave in and wrote to the guy telling him that he could change and that there was good in people. I explained how I forgave Ray. I ended up sending his wife a message on Facebook. I regret all of that now. I never received a reply from her, and I am so thankful I didn't.

Even though I was making mistakes, I finally felt like we were turning the corner and beginning to heal. I thought our family was going to be okay. Devyn went to prom in April 2017, and we all were there, except Josh. I was upset with Josh that he didn't make it but ended up blowing it off that he was twenty-one and living on his own now.

Chapter 24: Josh

On May 5, 2017, I messaged Josh and the conversation went like this:

You going to see me this weekend?

J: Doubt it.

Why not?

J: Bc I said

Ok? You mad at me?

J: I can't face you right now

Why? What did I do?

J: It's what I did

What did you do?

J: Not talking about it so stop

I told him he could tell me anything. I went on to just talk and tell him that I needed a fridge moved on Sunday and that I had a date that was local. I also jokingly told him I was going to kick his ass for not responding. On May 6, I messaged him and asked if he could please come and move the fridge. I told him if him and Tony could do it tomorrow that would be great. I didn't get any response.

On Sunday, May 7, I stopped by his house before church and told him that we were going out for lunch after church and would love to have him join us. He didn't say he would come but didn't say he wouldn't either. He had just woken up and his dark blonde hair was tousled. He was wearing athletic shorts and a shirt he had cut out the sleeves from. He was a country boy, through and through. Before I left, I told him I loved him.

Josh didn't come to lunch. That evening, Michael and I went to Casey's General Store and Josh was there. He came to the car window and talked to Mike and me for a bit. He said he was buying charcoal because his friends and him were going to barbeque that night. I noticed he was driving his best friend's car but didn't think anything about it. I assumed his friend's car was behind his truck, so he used it. He laughed at me because I had my hair in a ponytail and wearing a pink and white Bass Pro Shops hat that a guy had given me.

Monday, May 8, 2017

Monday morning was a typical day. I went to work at the newspaper, and I knew it would be a long day because I would be staying to cover the city meeting that evening. I knew I had a busy week ahead of me. Devyn was graduating from high school on Sunday, and I was planning a small party at the house after the graduation. It was an exciting time at our house.

That evening I headed to the city office in the town I worked in. I had my phone on silent, but I had it where I could see it if anyone called or text. I was always available for my kids. A number I didn't recognize appeared on the screen. I just ignored it and continued taking notes from the meeting. It appeared again and I started wondering if it was someone trying to get a hold of me about one of the kids. I thought it was Michael's summer ball coach or someone like that. I grabbed my phone and quietly stepped out of the city office to the front sidewalk and answered. I remember it was a nice evening out and it felt good to get out of the office for a minute.

The caller told me his name and I knew the name, but I wasn't connecting that he was the County Coroner. I was confused about why he was calling. He mentioned Josh and something had happened. I immediately wanted to know what hospital he was in, thinking there had been an accident and I needed to get to my son immediately. I don't remember his exact words, but he made it clear that Josh had shot himself and was gone. Life stopped. My chest ached as my heart broke into a million pieces. I couldn't breathe. I couldn't think. I am still unable to clearly remember the next few moments. I know I went back in the office, crying, and trying to get my stuff together. I barely remember the concerned faces of the mayor and alder persons sitting around the table. The chief of police drove me to the town Jake lived in, but I don't remember the drive. I remember pain. I remember hurt. I remember feeling like my life was ending. My sweet little blonde-haired, green-eyed, quiet little boy couldn't be gone. Josh was strong. He had grown to be six feet tall. I thought this had to be a mistake.

I remember being at Josh's house. Gary and Julie were there. There were cops and the coroner. All I wanted to do was go in and see Josh. I needed to see him. They wouldn't let me go in and that broke my heart. All I wanted was Josh. I understand why they wouldn't let me see him. Josh had used his white camouflage rifle to end his life. He put it under his chin and pulled the trigger. I realized later why they wouldn't let me in the house, but at that moment, I just wanted to see him. I wanted to kiss his cheek, touch his hand, tell him I loved him. I wanted it to all go away. I wanted him to walk out of the house.

I remember Lily arriving. She was running toward me, tears streaming down her cheeks, and pain etched on her face. As she got to the yard, she fell in the ditch, crying. The look of devastation and shock on her face broke my heart even more. Most of the evening was a blur. I remember the gurney coming out of the house and I knew that my son was in that black bag. I wanted to go to him. I didn't want that to be my last image of my beautiful boy. I wanted to at least touch his hand, tell him I love him, see part of him, at least one more time, but they had the bag zipped up and quickly took him away. There aren't words to describe the unimaginable pain that encompassed every part of me. I'm not even sure how I moved after that. The image will never leave my mind. It is burned in there forever. My beautiful boy's life was over, and he was moved from his house in a black bag. It hurt worse than anything.

I know that Gary talked to Michael and my mom and told them what had happened. I think Julie called Devyn. She was at her boyfriend's baseball game with his parents. It was over an hour away. Bailey was at college and some friends from church went to pick her up. We went to Gary and Julie's house, and I remember being in the driveway when Devyn arrived. Her boyfriend said she hadn't spoken the whole way home. She got out of the car and was just standing in the driveway. She was in complete shock. She didn't speak for a long time. She was in so much pain she couldn't move. She couldn't comprehend what was happening.

At some point that evening, I was back at my house to get things to go stay at Lily's house. I was moving in a robotic state. The pain was almost crippling, but I also knew that I needed to keep moving. I called the prison where Ray was at. I didn't want to talk to him. I didn't want him to call me later in the week. I wanted someone else to tell him. To be honest, I wanted him to hurt. There was a big part of me that blamed him in that moment. In that instant, I hated him and all the pain he had caused my family. The person I talked to told me they would have a pastor with him when they told him. I didn't care. I just wanted him to hurt.

We stayed at Lily's house that night. Bailey arrived later that evening and I don't think any of us slept. I couldn't stop crying. I was getting Facebook comments and messages from so many people, but I couldn't read them at that time. It was a very small community and word spread fast. I was dreading Tuesday. I was dreading going to the funeral home. I was dreading the finality of Josh being gone. There are not words to describe the pain a person feels when they lose a child. Every part of me was numb. The tears wouldn't stop. It was difficult to breathe, and my chest hurt. It felt like part of me was ripped away and I knew I would never be the same.

Chapter 25

Tuesday, I went home and took a shower, continuing to cry. Lily and I went to the funeral home. Planning a service for Jake was so difficult. I didn't know the answers. I had to provide words for an obituary. We had to come up with songs and details. We had to put together pictures and other mementos. We had to pick out an urn. A parent wasn't supposed to plan a child's funeral and a parent shouldn't have to pick out an urn to keep that child in. They are supposed to plan birthday parties, graduation parties, holidays, weddings, but not a funeral. I knew that I couldn't do two days, including a visitation and a funeral. We decided to have them both the same day, Monday, May 15. Devyn was to graduate high school on May 14, so I didn't want to do it before her graduation. I knew I had to try and make that day good for her despite all the pain our family was in. It was completely emotionally draining. We spent the rest of the day at Gary and Julie's house. Scott, our therapist, spent the day there. It was a comfort having him with us. He went above and beyond what was expected. He was a strong support that day.

Chapter 26

After Tuesday, all I wanted to do was sleep. I didn't want to face the pain or anyone. On Wednesday, Julie made me get up and out of bed. She reminded me that Devyn was graduating on Sunday, and I needed to get food for the get together I was having after her graduation. I also needed something to wear to the funeral on Monday. What do you wear for your child's funeral? I hated thinking about shopping for clothes for a funeral or anything else. I didn't want to go anywhere but I knew I had to for Devyn.

Julie took me shopping, and we got everything I needed. I hadn't eaten much since Monday and we went to Fazoli's for lunch. There was another store that Julie needed to stop at. Her twins were in Devyn's class, and she had a lot going on too, yet she was by my side every step of the way. When she went in the store, I decided to stay in the car. I was physically and emotionally drained and needed a few minutes alone in my grief. My phone rang. I immediately recognized the prison number. I answered and it was Ray. He acted normal. I was angry because I thought he had been told, and I couldn't figure out why he was acting so normal. He hadn't been told. I had to tell him. I remember him crying and that angered me. I told him I didn't want to hear him cry. It was a short conversation. I made it clear I didn't want to talk to him.

On Saturday, the women from church came to my house and cleaned and helped prepare food for Sunday. The men took care of moving my refrigerators and other things that needed done. I will forever be grateful for what my friends did. While everyone was inside working, I stepped outside, sit on my front porch, and watched my grandson, who was now three, play. I knew how much he loved Uncle Josh and he would miss him so much. Josh would take him fishing and to the park. They had a special bond. I had two hummingbird feeders out front that Josh had given me. They were glass orange ones and I loved them. Watching my grandson play and being so close to something special Josh had given me just continued to break my heart. Josh loved his family so much.

Text messages between Josh and I on March 2, 2017
Me: He (Lane) just said that he has had enough of your attitude.
J: Oh my goodness. I love that little boy so much.

Chapter 27

We lived in a small community, but I knew the school gymnasium would be packed for the graduation. I wanted this day to be about Devyn even though I knew we had Josh's death weighing heavy on all our hearts. I had told Gary that I didn't want people coming up to me talking about Josh because I knew I wouldn't be able to hold it together. I knew he told several people but there were still a few people who gave me their condolences. I knew they meant well, but I needed it to be about Devyn. During the graduation, the graduates presented their loved ones with roses. When Devyn gave me her rose, we hugged tightly, and we were both in tears. I could feel her holding on tightly and her pain was seeping into my heart. We gripped each other like our lives depended on each other, and at that moment, it did. This was her day, and we were crying because she was through with this phase of life and we were crying because we had so much pain losing Josh.

I hadn't had a chance that week to spend much time with my mom. She had been fighting cancer for seventeen years. She was in remission for several years and she seemed to be doing better at that time. But I think the death of Josh hit her hard. They had always been close. Friends brought her to the graduation, and she had to come in a wheelchair. She was seventy-seven but looked like she had aged a lot in the last week. She was so weak that it broke my heart. I made arrangements for someone to bring her to the funeral on Monday. It was hard because I felt like I couldn't take care of everyone like I wanted to.

We survived Sunday, but I was extremely exhausted. Several people stopped by the house to congratulate Devyn. Ray's mom and younger sister came to the graduation. I remember his sister telling me how sorry she was about what her family did to my family. It wasn't her fault and yet she felt the need to apologize because of what her brother had done. I was exhausted by the time everyone left, and Monday, the day of the funeral, was looming.

The visitation was first on Monday. There were so many people and it was exhausting talking to everyone. Devyn's boyfriend was on the baseball team, and they had an away game that day. The school allowed the bus to stop by the funeral home and the whole team and coaches came through the line and paid their condolences. It meant so much to Devyn and meant the world to our whole family. I don't remember the words people said to me or how I reacted. I remember the songs. I remember the pain my family felt. I remember deep pain. I remember my mom sitting beside me in a wheelchair. Her small frame slumped with her head leaning down. She was in pain.

The funeral followed the visitation. We had written letters to Josh and Gary read them at the funeral. People mentioned that it was a good service for Josh, but I was just angry there had to be a service at all. I was angry that Josh didn't talk to me, that I didn't see how bad he was hurting, that Ray hurt my children, and I was angry at God. I knew God wasn't the reason I lost Josh, and I came to realize through therapy that my anger and distance from God at that time stemmed from fear. I drew close to God after Ray was arrested and then I lost Josh. I was scared that if I remained close to God that something else bad would happen. I knew it was wrong. I knew that God didn't work that way, but I was scared to take that chance. I was angry at the world and I was angry at myself.

Letters to Josh

As *I write this, I'm not even sure what I should be writing about. I'm so confused by it all and I'll never understand why. All I can think about are the memories I had with you and all I can think about are the "no mores." No more driving your truck that you were nervous to let me drive because you seem to think I'm a crazy driver, no more sharing our favorite songs with each other, no more fishing, no more crazy selfies with you, no more coming home to you relaxing in the recliner, no more watching Greys Anatomy and me spoiling it for you, no more making fun of me and Kyle's relationship, no more of you eating all the leftover spaghetti and not saving any for me! No more flipping me off... which may sound crazy, but it is my favorite memory because you would always joke around with me and do it. Once I did it back, you told mom and she would never believe you because we all know I'm the angel child *winky face* I know this will be hard for me and I'll miss you like crazy, but I'll be here for my family when they need me just like you always said you would. Wish I could have told you that I loved you one last time. I always looked up to you because you really did have such a big heart and that's something I always try to have. I love you, big brother.*

Love your little sister,

Devyn

Dear Josh,

I miss you a lot and you were a good big brother. We always had fun together and there were some good memories like when we wrestled together, we played the X-box, you took me hunting and fishing, you took me out to eat, we played football together, and the best memory is when we jammed out to country music even though you're not a very good singer.

Your little brother,

Mike

Josh,

I wasn't really sure what to say because I'm a little bit angry at you right now, but we both know growing up we always seemed to be at each other's throats for something. Well, with the exception of that one time when we were little. I was at your chest, not your throat. We both know those weren't freckles on your chest; they were my teeth marks. My go to defense move probably shouldn't have been to bite you, but hey, it seemed to help at the moment. All joking aside, Josh, I'm heartbroken that you thought you had no other choice but this. Despite our constant go arounds, there's one thing I wish I would've shared with you so maybe, just maybe you didn't think this was your only option. And here it is: Our time here on earth is but "a few handbreadths." Psalm 39:5. This place is not our home, simply the pit stop before home. We are sojourners, guests, in this temporary dwelling place. There are trials that seem never ending, questions left unanswered, and pain that may never cease until we are home, but after all, there doesn't ever tend to be a road trip that is problem-free. For example, think about all of our family road trips. But in the end, no pain, trial, or struggle is worth taking your own life. Remember, there is hope, comfort, and deliverance when we turn to the One who sent his Son to make a way to a perfect, permanent, painless home.

Love,

Bailey

Josh,

This doesn't seem real. I miss you so much it hurts. I will forever cherish when you and Lane would run around mom's house being loud and pretending to wrestle. I love how you would let Lane get you down. He thinks he is big stuff because he got his big giant uncle down. I will miss you saying, "What's up old ladies?" to mom and me every time you came in. Lane is always telling me that he has to eat his bites so he can be big like Uncle Josh. You were always singing some old country song. I remember telling you to be quiet and ask who sings that song. Of course, you would say that you do and just sing louder. You were always pestering us. I love that you loved picking up Lane from daycare and then one time you took Lane fishing. Lane absolutely had a great time. Taking Lane on side-by-side rides is something that I will miss. Tony, Lane, and I love you so much. You were always willing to help Tony at the farm. You had such a kind heart. Even though you acted so tough, you were a big teddy bear. You were always talking about driving back roads, playing your music loud and having a cold one. Fly high, little brother. You are dearly missed.

Love,

Your big sister Lily

Josh,

I have so many questions that I may never have answers to. My mind is a mess. But the one thing I know for sure is how much I love you. When everything happened, less than two years ago, you were so strong and all you cared about was protecting your family. You loved us dearly. I know that. Your siblings meant the world to you and Lane was everything to you. I have so many memories to cherish. Remember puppy? You carried that stuffed toy in your mouth and everywhere. Grandma sewed it back together so many times. I still have it. I wanted to give it to your bride on your wedding day, but I won't get to do that now. I want to touch on more recent memories. Remember in November, when you took me hunting? Sitting in the deer stand with you is one of my favorite memories. There was our two-day trip in December. You shared your heart, Josh. You opened up about so much and it was two of the greatest day with you. How about the day a few months ago when I told you I thought something was wrong with my car? You told me that I needed a wobinator shaft. You kept a straight face while I \Googled it. I was unable to find it and was prepared to call the mechanic to price a wobinator shaft. You finally told me there was no such thing. You got a good laugh out of that. Who is going to aggravate me in the kitchen and eat all the Velveeta? Who is going to laugh at me shooting the shotguns? Who am I going to make fun of when the Sooners lose and who will give me a hard time when the Cardinals lose?

You picked up Lane one day not too long ago and took him to the park. I stopped by because it was a warm day and I wanted to make sure you had a drink for him. You had already been to Casey's. You were pushing him in the swing, and he was so happy. He loved you Josh. My favorite recent memory was a few weeks ago. You were worried about me dating again and you became worse than a parent. You grabbed my face with both hands and made me look you in the eyes. You told me I was a beautiful person and that I didn't need a man because no one would be good enough for your mother. You were so serious that day. I know how much you cared.

As angry and confused as I am, I find my hope and comfort in Christ. I know He was with you in those final moments. I know His heart broke, and He held you when I couldn't. I know you knew the truth of God's Word and that you are with Him now. I know I will see you again. I'm angry. I'm hurt. But I know where my true comfort comes from. I will hold on to my anchor in Christ. I know He held you. I love you. I will miss you every day. I will see you again, my son.

Love,

Mom (Old Lady)

Chapter 28

After the funeral, we were in the car in front of the funeral home. I remember Tony, my son-in-law, holding my grandson outside the car and Lane started crying. He wanted Uncle Josh. He was too young to understand what happened, but he knew Josh was gone. He had been good through the funeral, and a three-year-old can't begin to understand what was going on. But, when we got outside, something clicked for him, and he knew, in only a way a child could know, that his Uncle Josh wasn't there. It was heart wrenching to see a three-year-old so devastated.

Lane is now seven and he has a very sensitive heart, a lot like Josh. He talks about Josh and remembers time with him. He likes to watch videos and see pictures of them together. He is now asking more questions about Josh's death. We haven't told him how Josh died and still struggling with how to tell him, but we know we need to share the truth with him eventually.

A local café provided a meal for us after the funeral, and we gathered there to eat. It took everything I had within me to eat and not fall completely apart. After I got home, I crawled into bed and collapsed from exhaustion. I hadn't been home long when Josh's biological father text me and wanted Josh's truck. I was devastated. We just had our son's funeral, and he didn't even speak to me there and now all he wanted was Josh's truck. I knew how Josh felt about his dad and I talked to the other kids. We knew the last person Josh would want to have his truck was his dad, so I decided we would keep it for now. I had spoken to him after Josh's death and he told me that he had spoken to Josh the night before he took his life. He said Josh was mad at him and they argued. I may never know what had Josh so angry that night, but I couldn't think about his belongings at that time. It was too much.

Journal Entry August 23, 2015 (almost two years before his death)
Last night Josh got into an argument with his dad. His dad wants to cause me problems. Then he threatened to kick Josh's ass. Who says that to their kid? Lord, I pray he backs off too.

Chapter 29

Tuesday morning, I sit at my dining room table looking at all the cards, envelopes, flowers, and stuff from the funeral. I didn't have any energy to think about going through that stuff. I was emotionally and physically exhausted and I missed Josh so much. My phone rang and it was my mom. She said the ambulance was taking her to the emergency room. I was devastated. I was barely functioning and now I had to figure this out. I called Lily and she came and picked me up and we went to the emergency room. Mom was so weak, and we knew she wouldn't be able to go back to her apartment. I was upset with myself knowing that I didn't have energy to move her in with me. She was admitted to the hospital and we talked to the social worker about getting mom into a nursing home to regain her strength so she could come back to her apartment.

During the two weeks of losing Josh, Devyn's graduation, and Mom going to the hospital, our cat got ran over and both of Devyn's dogs went missing. I didn't know how much more our family could take. I was ready to just give up, but somehow, I got up each day and kept moving. I went back to work on Thursday, May 18. I was a single mom and had to have an income. I didn't get child support because Ray was in prison, so I knew I had to get back into a normal routine.

After I lost Josh, I tried to ignore the guys who were still messaging me. I didn't want to deal with that, but the messages just kept coming. My anger was all-consuming, and I wanted to numb the pain. I once again went down that dangerous road of not caring about myself. Again, I used guys, and I was used. I didn't care what happened to me. I just wanted the pain to end. I was having a hard time functioning and being around people. I didn't veer toward drug and alcohol. I went to sex. I thought sex could numb my pain, but it only added to it. I was a complete mess. I cried a lot. I didn't want to be around people. I didn't want to do anything because everything hurt.

My mom moved into the nursing home the following Saturday and I felt overwhelmed dealing with that too. I couldn't even take her to the nursing home. A friend picked her up from the hospital and took her to the nursing home. I ended up going and spending the day with a guy. It was easier than facing life. I felt like I was failing everyone. God, my friends, my children, my mother, everyone.

Chapter 30

Journaling had been a lot of therapy for me but in the last few months I was so wrapped up in dating and school that I hadn't written in it for a long time. I wrote in it on May 12, 2017.

Monday, May 8, was the worst day ever. I thought when I found out what Ray did, it was the worst. But, no getting a call from the coroner while you are in a city meeting is the most unimaginable. Then to find out your son took his life… I'm pissed. I'm angry. I'm hurt. I'm confused. I don't understand. God, I want to know why. Why didn't you stop him? Why did you take him from me? Why was he so upset? I want answers. Where are the damn answers? My heart is broken. How do you move past this? Lord, how do I? I know I have been distance. I have been focused more on sex. I know that, but why did Josh have to be taken from me? I can't understand. So many people have helped, and I know they don't have the words to tell me. I know they try. I feel smothered. Then when I am alone, it is quiet, and I am scared. I can't sleep well. I miss him so much. I worry about the kids. Mike doesn't say much. He acts like everything is normal except when he is mean to me. God, I know I need you, but I'm void of emotion except pain and anger. I am angry at you, and I want you to comfort me, but I don't know how to draw close to you because I am a sinner. God, I miss him so much. Did he know you? Did he reach out for you? Is he with you now? God, please, I need to know. Lord, please let me know that you are with me. Please let me feel you. Please forgive me. Why did Josh do this? Why did he leave me? I don't want to be angry that he felt he had no other options, but I am. I am really angry at Ray. I forgave him but now I don't know what to think. How could he hurt my kids? How do I now protect Mike? I couldn't protect Josh. I lost him. I didn't protect him. Why couldn't I protect him from the abuse and from taking his life? I miss him. I love him. I don't want him to be gone. Why? Why? Why, Lord? I can't comprehend. I can't understand why he felt this was his only answer. What do I do now? How do I draw closer to you? How do I make sure Devyn has a good graduation Sunday? I can't do any of this. It hurts too much. Lord, please help me. Please, Lord. I need you.

Over the next few weeks, we had to get Josh's truck from his house. It was completely out of gas. I found out that he had quit his job several weeks ago and had no money in his account. I was shocked that he hadn't told any of us. Everyone thought he was still going to work every day. His friend that he lived with thought he was still working. He went to work before Josh and got home after him, so he assumed he was still working. His friend was the one who heard the gunshot when he got home from work on May 8. He was still outside the house and when he heard it, he ran to the sheriff's department. They lived behind the post office, which was on the square across from the courthouse, on the other side of the square from the newspaper office.

We met the landlord at the house because we needed to get his belongings out of the house, but I couldn't go inside. Lily went inside the house, and it was very hard on her. I was too weak to go inside. I felt like I failed again.

A classmate and friend of Lily's worked at a funeral home in Columbia. She came and washed all of Josh's clothes and went through his belongings. Josh's Bible was found next to him on the bed, where he was sitting the day he took his life. Lily's friend cleaned it and even though the pages are still blood-stained, it is a precious possession to me. I kept it in his orange and camouflage Bible case in a curio cabinet I had full of Josh's stuff. I struggled with the image of Josh sitting on the bed with his rifle, alone and scared. That image rips my heart in half. After I found out that he had his Bible next to him, I had a little comfort knowing that, hopefully, he had cried out to God in his last moments. I need to believe that Jesus was with him at that time. Otherwise, him being alone and terrified will eat at me for the rest of my life. He had to be scared, sad, angry. What was going through his mind? Was he crying? He was alone in that painful moment. I am his mom, and I wasn't there for him. Mothers are supposed to protect their kids when they are scared. They are supposed to comfort them and tell them everything will be okay. It hurts knowing how alone Josh was that day.

Lily and I tried to go to grief classes, but I couldn't embrace what anyone was saying. I was too angry and had too much pain that I couldn't let go of. One thing I did learn though was that grief is a very personal thing and no one can judge you or tell you how to experience grief. It is yours. Embrace it and go through it however you need to. I'm not saying I didn't make mistakes with my grief, because I did, but it was still my grief. The pain never goes away. Songs, memories, or a word or phrase will bring the tears.

Lily and Tony put gas in Josh's truck so we could move it. They found a notebook under the driver's seat. He had written a letter to the family. There was a note to me, Lily, Tony, Bailey, Devyn, Michael, and Lane. It was obvious how much Josh loved us, but it was obvious how much pain he was in. His letter didn't clear up a lot, but he did say that he didn't want to end up like his biological dad and that he was upset about things he had done. He made it sound like a girl he had been with was pregnant, but we have no way of knowing for sure. It weighs heavily on me wondering if Josh has a child out there. My grandchildren are my world, so the thought of another one being out there, is hard to handle. I don't know if I will ever know.

The end of the letter mentioned that we shouldn't blame Ray because he was a good dad, except for what he did. The sad part is that Josh was manipulated into thinking Ray was different even through death. I can't help but blame Ray. I still believe if Ray wouldn't have sexually abused Josh, Lily, and Michael, that Josh would still be here today. It is a domino effect. What Ray did changed and impacted our family forever. He can never take that back.

Josh's letter

Dear Family,

I just want you to know I love you more then words can describe. I just want to thank you so much for always being here for me. The best family a guy could ever ask for. I'm just not happy. Nothing ever works out in my favor. I'm a screwup. I'm tired of my feelings getting played with. IDK what to really say. I just have done some pretty sick things in my life and have lately. It has been getting to me. I deserve what I did to myself. I'm just tired of everything. I'm broke. I wouldn't even be able to make my truck payment. I'm tired of giving my all into a girl that acts like they care but them don't. I just got taken advantage of. I'm tired of it. It know it is selfish and a cowardly way out, but I have to do it. All the things I have done are hitting me pretty hard. Hopefully I don't end up being a dad after doing this. It's a good possibility but _____ hates me now, so who cares if she gets pregnant. I can't do it any longer. I'm sorry I have failed you guys.

Mom, thank you for always being here for me, no matter what. You are the best mom a son could ever ask for. I love you, mom.

Tony, thank you brother for teaching me a lot of things and helping me out. I truly looked up to you. Take care of my sister and nephew. I know you will, but I'll remind you always. Thank you, bro. Love ya.

Lily, You're an awesome mother. I couldn't ask for a better big sister besides you. You have a beautiful family and I hope your family grows. Lane couldn't ask for a better mother than you. Thank you for everything. I love you Lily.

Bailey, I know we have barely talked the last four years and I'm sorry for that. I have always loved you like you was blood. You're doing an awesome job in college. I'm proud of you. Keep up the hard work. I love you B.

Devyn, You have turned into quite the young lady. I wish I would have been more like you when I was younger. You are truly a blessing to this family. When we were all down you know the right thing to say to lighten the mood. You are going to go very far in life. Be safe at college. I love you D.

Michael, I love you. I know I didn't say it more like I should but I couldn't have asked for a better little brother. Please listen to mom and keep a good attitude. You don't wanna end up like me. Do your schoolwork. You're gonna be a good athlete when you get older. Hit the gym, beef up, and you will be set. I love you, bro.

Lane, I love you little buddy. You are my world. I wouldn't know what to do without you. Be a good boy. I'll be looking down on you and watching out for you, little buddy. Uncle Goshua loves you, little buddy.

I know this is all confusing, but I'm so messed up. I can't continue being a burden on everyone. Please tell dad I love him. He was the best dad a kid could ask for besides what he did. Tell grandma I love her and thank her for everything. I'm just so messed up in the head right now. I can't think straight. Please do not blame this on anyone or yourselves. It's 100% my fault. I love you all and I'll be watching out for you all wherever I end up.

Love,

Josh

Journal Entry August 25, 2015

Today, Josh opened up about how he feels. He loves Ray and he misses him but hates him too. It made me feel better to hear him say that because I feel so guilty for loving him. He wants to face him and yell at him and then have a normal conversation with him too. I understand all of that. It has to be so much harder for Josh and Michael because they knew a really bad side that I didn't know. I wish I knew the answers.

The part of Josh's letter where he talks about loving Ray and the journal entry above both show how we all still lived on that line of loving Ray and hating what he did. We all struggled with reconciling the person we thought with the person that did this. It didn't help that he knew us well enough to know how to manipulate our feelings and make us believe that he was a good person. I'm not saying people can't change. With God, anyone can change. I'm not saying that we shouldn't forgive, but I'm saying that I don't believe that Ray has truly accepted the full responsibility for what he has done. He still writes letters to people from the county we lived in, and some of those people are not ones he talked to on a regular basis. I believe it is his way of making people believe he is a good person.

Josh loved the family so much and was a big help with both Michael and Lane.

March 17, 2017 Text messages
Me: Please, with sugar on top, pick up Michael at school at 4:30. He has track practice. I will figure out next week but have no way to get him today.
J: Okay. That's fine. I gotta run to the house anyway today.
J: And can I take a few old pans or pots you don't use much of
Me: Yes, just be sure they aren't what I use.
J: Duh lol.
Me: Smart donkey.
J: Smart what

March 28, 2017
J: Ya gonna be home tonight
Me: Yep. You coming over for supper?
(Hours later when my fear took over)

Me: What is your deal? You asked if I was going to be home so I thought you were coming over or something but you haven't answered me. Trying to worry me?

J: I was but I fell asleep. Just woke up. Chill woman.

Me: Oh lol! I thought something happened to you.

J: Are you home?

Me: Well of course.

J: I'll probably head your way.

April 4, 2017 (Clue about his financial situation)

Me: It is pizza night.

J: I'm broke.

Me: I will buy.

J: No.

Me: Why not?

J: Bc I'm not letting you do that.

Me: I offered.

J: Still

Me: Still what? I'm sure sometime in the future you can take me out.

J: Noooooooo

April 7, 2017

J: Wanna go for a run tonight?

Me: I've been using elliptical but I could run.

J: Good.

Me: Getting a tattoo at the moment.

J: Excuse me. What are you getting and where at?

A couple of months before we lost Josh, we had an incident with children's division. Mike, from the time he was little, would break out with a rash anytime he was near weeds. He loved to be outside chasing frogs, fishing, and playing near the creek. When he was younger, we took him to a dermatologist and provided them pictures of his rash. We had cream to put on it when it would happen and would usually have to take him to the doctor for a steroid shot.

Mike broke out after playing outside when he was thirteen and broke out in a rash on his arms, abdomen, and chest. He refused his cream and would pick at it. It spread to his neck and face and by the weekend his face was really swollen. On Sunday, I considered taking him to the emergency room but he was feeling fine and not in any respiratory distress. I monitored him closely. Monday morning, there was no change, so he went to school, and I made him a doctor's appointment when I got to work.

That morning I received a call from the school nurse and she wanted me to come get him and take him at that time. I explained that I had made him a doctor's appointment and would pick him up in the afternoon to take him. It was a Monday, and I had to get the paper layout finished so it could be sent for print. I was working in my office when a caseworker from children's division came in. I knew her from when we did foster care and we lived in a very rural area. She said I had to take him to the doctor sooner. I was shocked that the school made a hotline call when I had an appointment for him. I worked closely with the school with my job at the newspaper, all my kids had gone there, and I went to church with the principal.

I don't blame the school now, and I respect the job they have. I realize they were doing what they thought was best, but at the time, it was one more stressor I didn't need.

I tried to tell the caseworker that he had an appointment, but she was adamant that I call and see if I could get him in earlier. I called the doctor's office and they said they would try and fit him in earlier than his appointment.

Fuming, I left work, went to the school and picked up Mike who was in no distress. Yes, his face was red and swollen and he looked bad, but this was something we had dealt with for years and I knew what to watch for. We went to the doctor and waited in the waiting room forever. Mike played games on the phone while we waited. He ended up being seen, and receiving his shot, five minutes before his actual appointment time.

Since an investigation was open, Josh and Devyn had to be interviewed. When I told Josh, he was very angry. Josh always felt like he had to be the man of the house and protect me and his siblings. He couldn't believe, after what we had went through, that we would have to go through this too. Of course, nothing came of the investigation and it was unsubstantiated but it was one more thing that added to our family's fragile emotional state.

February 27, 2017

Me: After I already told them Michael had a doctor appointment this afternoon, DFS showed up at work and made me leave then to take him and they are going to follow up. I'm so mad.

J: Are you f***ing kidding me?

Me: Wish I was.

J: DFS better hope I don't cross paths with them. That's bullshit.

Chapter 31

Growing up, Josh was a quiet kid. He had a big heart and was sensitive. When he was little, he had blonde hair that curled in the back like a ducktail. I remember when I decided to cut his hair. It was needed but broke my heart. He looked so grown up after it was cut.

When I met Ray, they seemed to instantly bond. Josh was almost three and we had his third birthday at Ray's house. Josh was so happy. We moved to southern Missouri before we got married and then came back to our area for our wedding. Josh was our ring bearer and Bailey and Lily, along with another little girl were our flower girls. When it was time for Josh and Bailey to walk down the aisle, Josh was nervous. When he saw Ray standing at the altar, he grabbed Bailey's hand and dragged her down the aisle. Everyone laughed. I didn't get to see it, but everyone said it was hilarious.

Josh was shy but had an infectious smile. When he turned four, he wanted a sheep and I remember how much he loved "Cottonball." He was in preschool and Ray was going to be the Easter Bunny at an event at his school. Josh knew it was his dad under the costume and even though his smile reached for miles, he never told any of the other kids that it wasn't the "real" Easter Bunny.

We lived in southern Missouri for a year and then moved back to Northeast Missouri. I missed my family and hated living so far away. Josh and Bailey were very close when they were little. They were only seven months apart so people would think they were twins. All three kids were so excited when Devyn was born. Josh was a good brother and loved his sisters so much. As the kids grew up, Josh became more of a country kid. He would probably call himself a redneck. He loved to hunt and fish. In his short adult years, he loved driving back roads, drinking a beer, bonfires, and his boots. It was rare to see him in tennis shoes when he got older.

In the middle of Josh's junior year of high school, he quit football. His equipment was in his vehicle and Ray told him he had to get it returned to the school. Josh was mad and the next thing I knew he left, and I didn't know where he went. He called later and had moved in with his biological dad. I was devastated because he didn't like his dad that much. He was angry with us and I couldn't figure out why. I took him some of his stuff and met him at the lake one day. We sit and talk, and he never would give me an explanation of why he moved there. Lane was born

November 2013 and I was so happy that Josh came to the hospital that day. He still wouldn't come home. He spent part of his junior year and his senior year at his dad's house.

Josh graduated in May 2014 and he invited us to his graduation. Ray, Lily, Lane, and I went. I was so proud of Josh that day. It wasn't long after that before he moved back home. He never said why he moved from our home or why he came back. He only said it was a mistake and that he doesn't want anything to do with his biological dad. I didn't realize at that time, he probably left because of the abuse that was happening to him.

During my disastrous dating phase, Josh and Lily's dad text me and we started talking. We met one night when I was covering a ball game for the paper. After the game, I went to the agreed location and I got in his truck. The moment I got in, I knew it was a mistake and that I had no feelings for this man, not even a bit of attraction to him. I tried to close everything off and make it about sex. We didn't have sex in his truck, but we kissed and talked about getting together again. I didn't want the kids to know we were talking, so we agreed not to tell them. That night we sent some messages that were sexual in nature, but I knew I couldn't go down that road. I also knew that I didn't like keeping secrets from my kids, especially after what our family had gone through with Ray. I told Josh, and he exploded in anger. I couldn't understand why he was so mad. I thought he was mad at me, but he wasn't. He was mad because he didn't want his dad anywhere around me. He was trying to protect me.

I didn't talk to his dad again until we lost Josh. We didn't speak at the funeral. He came with his girlfriend, other children, and I did give him pictures of Josh, but we didn't speak. He text me after the funeral about the truck and the next time I heard from him was a few weeks later when I was at the doctor. I was waiting on results of a breast biopsy I had recently had done. I was terrified that something else bad was going to happen and that I had cancer. Thankfully, everything was okay. But, when I was sitting in the waiting room, I was scared. Josh's dad started texting me and cussing me because I wouldn't let him have Josh's truck. He blamed me for Josh's death and said a lot of mean things. It seemed like he never cared about Josh, but only cared about what materialistic items he could get.

Memories of Josh would continue to play in my mind every day. I would call his phone just to hear his voice. I was so worried I would forget what he sounded like. I would watch videos on my phone. One video was where he was aggravating Lily by hiding her phone and she was chasing him around the house with a broom, while Lane followed them around. It was a night that Josh was happy, and I still watch it many times.

One thing about Josh I will never forget was his fierce protectiveness of those he cared for. Scott, our therapist, said that Josh had a protective nature and that he would do anything to protect those he loved. I wonder if he didn't think he was protecting us by ending his life. If only he would have known that we would have been there for him, and would have tried to protect him from what he did, would things have been different?

Chapter 32

One day, after I started dating, and found out it wasn't very easy, I was in the house cooking lunch and Josh and Lily were both in the kitchen. Lily was sitting on the sink and Josh was stealing the Velveeta as I cut it for the macaroni and cheese. We were talking about my latest dating fiasco and Josh grabbed my face, hands on both cheeks, and though he towered over me, he looked me directly in my eyes and said, "Mom, you're beautiful inside and out. You don't need those jerks." I tried to laugh it off, but he was serious, and I could see the sincerity in his green eyes. There is no doubt how much Josh cared about his family. The warmth of his hands on my cheeks that day will never be forgotten.

Josh didn't open up much about the abuse. I'm not sure if he discussed it much in therapy, but he didn't say much to us. Josh worked nights, and one Saturday morning, he woke me up when he got home from work and said he was taking me to breakfast. I wanted to sleep, but I knew it meant the world to him. We had a good breakfast and we had a good talk. I did ask Josh about the abuse and all he said was, "Mom, you don't want to know. All I can say is that it was worse than you can imagine." I will never completely know what Josh went through. The only person who knows what my beautiful son went through is the person in prison that I never want to speak to again.

Chapter 33

It took a long time after losing Josh to go through his clothes and his room. He hadn't taken everything when he moved so he still had quite a bit of stuff in his room. Josh was an Oklahoma Sooners and Chicago Bears fan. He had a lot of that type of clothing. I kept a lot of his favorite items and got rid of the rest. It was very painful to let anything go. Josh had to be cremated and I had his ashes on top of the cabinet that was full of some of his belongings.

One of my favorite things that belonged to Josh is a small stuffed cat. When he was a toddler, it was given to him as a gift. He loved that toy. He would call it "puppy." He took it everywhere and would carry it in his mouth by one ear when he was playing. He slept with it every night. One night Josh was in his crib and started crying, "Puppy, puppy. I need puppy." We had no idea where it was at. We looked everywhere in the house and his dad ended up finding it outside. When we handed it to Josh, he cuddled it against his tear-streaked face, and sighed, "Puppy." He was instantly asleep. My mom spent many hours sewing ears back on, the tail back on, and stitching puppy up. I kept it with plans to give it to Josh's bride at his wedding. There will never be a wedding for Josh. He will never get to show puppy to his kids. Puppy will never be with the boy that loved the toy unconditionally for years. Puppy looks rough, but puppy was loved more than most toys by an adorable blonde haired, green-eyed boy.

After I lost Josh, I didn't want to be angry with him, but I was. I was angry at him for not telling me how much he was hurting. I was angry at him for taking his life so close to Devyn's graduation. I was angry at him for not thinking about how much Lane loved him. Of course, that anger caused me to feel guilty.

I have to wonder if Josh didn't suffer from depression. The abuse, the guilt, the pain, and the frustration had to be hard for him to process. I remember one night that he was out drinking and had his gun with him. I wonder now if he wasn't contemplating suicide at that time. I can't remember if his girlfriend and he were still together or had broken up, but I remember talking to her that night, and she wanted me to call the cops. I was concerned that he would get in trouble or do something stupid if I did that. He wouldn't respond to my text messages. I finally told him I was going to call the cops and then he wrote me back and told me he was fine and would be home in the morning. I didn't sleep, but Josh did come home. He never talked about what was wrong or what happened. I blew it off as having too much to drink, but now I wonder if it wasn't a cry for help. I don't think there will be a day that goes by that I don't wonder if there was something different that could have been done to save him.

I think about his letter a lot and wonder when he wrote it. I saw him on Sunday, the day before, and talked to him twice. Did he know? Had he already written the letter? When did he put it in his truck? Was he planning this or was it a last-minute decision? I may never have the answers to those questions. I do know that he mentioned some things to a lady he rode with to work that made her question his thoughts and if he had been planning. She came and visited with us after we lost Josh. She told me how much Josh loved me and would do anything for me. She said that Josh had quit his job in April, yet none of us knew. The signs of his mindset may have been all around us and we missed them. You never think it could happen to your family, but it can. I can't go back and change the past. I wish I could.

Chapter 34

Grief doesn't disappear. It changes as time goes by, but it is never gone. There are days when it is worse than other days. I was doing homework one day and missing Josh overcame everything I was doing. I love to write, mostly suspense fiction novels, but that day I wrote a poem. I don't claim to be good at poetry but what came out was grief, raw and real. I didn't mean to write a poem, but the words started flowing. When I started seeing Scott for therapy, he told me to journal since I liked writing. Journaling was very therapeutic for me.

My Grief

The sky is bright blue with wisps of white clouds
A gentle breeze stirs, warm and comforting
I feel it on my skin, soft, gentle
It is always there, a memory, bittersweet
Sometimes as gentle as a summer breeze

The day turns to gray as rumbles are heard
The wind picks up whipping my hair
The storm is brewing outside and inside
As the memories begin to hurt my heart
I miss the gentle breeze, soft and gentle

The sky is black as the tornado moves closer
The winds are now painful, agonizing
I want to run from it, but it is circling around me
Tossing me here and there
Making it impossible to breathe

It hurts
It angers me
It confuses me
It brings the tears
It is more than I can bear

It was that song on the radio
The one that played the day we said goodbye
The one that always reminds me of you
It isn't only that song that brings the pain
Sometimes it is a word, a phrase, a picture, a moment in time.

I don't like the days the tornado comes
I don't like feeling this way
I don't like the tears that leak down my face
I don't like the hollow emptiness in my heart
I don't like when people tell me it is only a phase

How do they know I will get better?
This is personal to me
Who invented the stages of grief?
No one should tell me how I feel today
They can't know what memory will stir the winds

My second-born, my son
You were my boy
Now all I have is memories
I worry I will forget your voice
I can't do that; I can't forget anything about you

You had an infectious laughter
You had a big heart
You were a protector of your family
You were quirky and fun
You were a son, brother, uncle, and friend.

The moment you picked up that gun
You took a piece of my heart with you
You were hurting and in pain
I'm sorry I didn't know
Wasn't there another option?

This is my grief
No one can tell me how to experience it
There are days that it is a gentle breeze
But when the wind begins to blow harder
The storm rages

My mood changes
The memories hurt
My heart aches
I don't want to do today
This is my grief.

Chapter 35

I think most people think of suicide as a selfish act. I thought that. But I don't think Josh committed suicide out of selfishness. I think he committed suicide out of pain and a necessity to protect those he loved. Josh had a very protective nature. Scott said Josh would have continued taking any abuse just to keep the family together and happy. When he found out it happened to his siblings, he had so much guilt. Everyone tried to tell him it wasn't his fault. It was Ray's fault, but Josh couldn't move past the guilt he felt. I wish I could say Josh's letter answered our question "why" and cleared up a lot of confusion, but it didn't. It did show how much he cared about us, how much he didn't want to be like his biological dad, and how much he didn't like the person he was. As wrong as it is, I think Josh thought he was protecting us by leaving us.

Many people say that people who commit suicide go to Hell. I don't believe that. I believe Josh is in Heaven. I believe in those final moments he cried out to God. I believe that Jesus was with him. After I lost Josh, someone recommended a CD called Chaos of the Heart. It was made by Music for the Soul. It is a combination of songs and talking. The songs encompassed so many of my emotions. I listened to them a lot. One thing that stuck with me was during some of the speaking parts on the CD, a guy talked about how people commit suicide don't go to Hell. I remember them telling analogies about people who were saved but might commit sin right before they die. It brought up this question in my mind, "If you don't get a chance to repent of a sin before death, will you automatically go to Hell?" I don't think so. I think God knows the heart. I believe God knows the person intimately and I believe he knew Josh's heart and that Josh is in Heaven watching over us.

Chapter 36

Losing someone to suicide is confusing and painful. When people ask me how many kids I have, I still answer, "five." The hard part is when they ask their ages. I can give them Lily's age, Bailey's age, Devyn's age, and Michael's age. When it comes to Josh, I have to say, "Well, he would have been… this year. We lost him in 2017."

"Oh, I'm sorry. What happened?"

"He committed suicide."

Awkward silence.

Suicide and mental illness carry a stigma and people have a hard time grasping what to say in those situations. As things change in our society, I can only pray and hope that stigma disappears.

I currently work as a school-based health centers nurse and work with mental health. I attend a lot of suicide conferences and mental health webinars. I wish I would have had some of this knowledge before losing Josh. I think it is important that people open up about mental health and suicide. We shouldn't be afraid to ask others how they are feeling. We can't be afraid to mention the word "suicide." If a person is truly considering suicide, asking them about it is not going to make them go out and do it sooner. It will open the door to important conversations that might save their lives.

I recently decided that I want to help spread the word about suicide, help people understand the myths, the truths, the stigmas, and help survivors. I am going to volunteer for the Missouri chapter of the American Foundation for Suicide Prevention (AFSP). After attending a virtual conference at work and learning more about their beliefs and programs, I am passionate about working with them and have sent an application.

Chapter 37

The pain never went away, and I continued to try to mask it with inappropriate behavior and I hated myself for it. I have always been a person committed to one person and loves with all my heart. I didn't love or care for any guy I was with; I just wanted to feel nothing. I pretended to care about some of the guys I was dating, but I didn't. I even reciprocated "I love you." But it wasn't real. It was a way to not think about the grief, a way to not feel the all-consuming pain that woke me up at night, the pain that tore pieces of my heart away.

The end of July 2017, I went out with two friends from high school for a few drinks and a girl's night out. All three of us have July birthdays and we were celebrating that. We were reminiscing about high school days and one of my friends asked me if I had ever connected with James, my high school boyfriend for two years, and the one I took to my junior prom. Before my senior year, my family moved from Missouri to Arizona. This was the 80s, so we didn't have cell phones and easy ways to stay connected. We came back home to visit at Christmas and James and I spent some time together. He had already graduated, and he wanted me to stay in Missouri with him. I said I would, but I didn't. I still had my senior year to finish and went back to Arizona with my family. We hadn't spoken since then and I didn't realize how much I hurt him.

I had tried to find him on Facebook several times and even messaged a guy with the same name, but it wasn't him. My friend said she had been friends with him on Facebook for a long time and that I should add him. I was a little apprehensive because it had been twenty-eight years since I had seen him and if he wanted to talk to me, why hadn't he looked for me. But, after a few more drinks, I requested him as a friend and didn't think much more about it.

The next day, I received a message from James. We started talking and the years melted away. He told me that he gave me his heart in high school and had never taken it back. At that time, he was in Florida with two of his kids and his ex-wife, but he said he didn't like living there and was already planning to come back to Missouri. I didn't want to be the reason he came back to Missouri because I would never want to come between a relationship, so we kept things casual, even though we both had feelings. We decided to just be friends. I was dating a guy in Missouri, and he was there, so I never expected anything to come out of it.

Then one day he messaged me and said that he was coming back to Missouri and the day he would be back. I gave him my phone number but didn't realize until later that I didn't have his phone number. It was a Wednesday, and I had a school board meeting to cover for the paper that night. I kept thinking I would get a message that he was home but never heard anything. I had accepted that he had changed his mind and wasn't coming back to Missouri. I had broken up with the guy I was dating, but not because of James. I was already planning on ending things because he was getting more serious than I wanted. I was pretending to care and pretending to be serious with him. It wasn't fair to him.

I went to bed that night with a heavy heart because the only guy who had sparked any real emotion in me since my divorce was in Florida and not coming back to Missouri. My phone rang and it was a number I didn't recognize but I answered it. It was James, and he was back in Missouri. He had moved back, and he was at his parents. He said he would call me the next day. I was excited and terrified. What if our feelings weren't still there when we saw each other? What if this was just another way for me to mask my grief?

We talked on Thursday, and we made plans to meet on Friday evening. I was nervous but excited. I arrived at our meeting place first and he shortly pulled up behind me. We both got out of our vehicles and hugged each other for the longest time. The years melted away and I felt like we had never been apart. I was scared to have feelings for anyone. I had spent most of my time not feeling. I was just numbing the pain with sex and companionship. I wasn't sure I wanted to feel. I wasn't sure I could love again.

We talked a lot about the past. I was amazed that he remembered so many details about our high school relationship and I was shocked that he remembered exactly what I was wearing the day he saw me when we were back for Christmas break. He told me how much I hurt him because he asked me to stay with him in Missouri and not go back to Arizona. I didn't realize how bad I had hurt him. It was strange for me how so many feelings came back to me but there were also new adult feelings that I hadn't felt for a long time.

James met my kids and we spent almost every day together. I never planned to get married again. He had only been married once, and it had been a long time ago. He had relationships but was used to being single. I had been married twice and had serious trust and insecurity issues. But we loved each other and knew we wanted to be together. I was finally feeling again and not trying to pretend to be happy with someone. On September 15, 2017, we got married at the courthouse and planned to have a reception later. We decided to go ahead and sell my house and move to where James was from. I thought the change might be good for Mike;

starting a new school where no one knew about his past, about the abuse, about his brother's suicide.

Chapter 38

The last time I spoke to Ray was shortly after James and I were married. I told him to not call me again. He still called Lily a lot and it would upset her, but she is a lot like me and would answer the phone because she would feel bad. Then all he would talk about is himself and how prison is and how horrible the food is. I wrote him a letter and asked him to leave my family alone. The calls and letters to Lily stopped for a little while but started back up again. I wrote to him in the fall of 2020 and was very blunt that we didn't want to talk to him. I sent the letter to Lily, and she was glad I was sending it. But he called her again and then he sent the girls money for Christmas. I'm not sure where he got money when he owes a lot in back child support. I didn't want them to take the money because it is his way of getting them to talk to him, but I knew they could all use it, and it wasn't my place to tell them not to take it.

I hope someday that Lily sees how he is manipulating her like he did me. I know she struggles with the fact that both her dads were not good people. I remember her telling me one time that I shouldn't miss Ray because I have them and that should be enough. I wish she would see that she has so many people that love her and that is all she needs.

Even through all of Ray's confessions, I realized he still lied. He said the abuse stopped when Lily was very young. Lily had blocked out a lot of the abuse but over the years, memories have come back to her and the abuse went on a lot longer than he said. Josh's abuse lasted over eight years and Mike had been abused for two years before he told what happened. I believe that Ray truly thinks he is different than other people that molest kids. But he is worse because he doesn't recognize how horrible the things are that he did. He doesn't seem to realize that what he did caused so many other tragedies and painful moments.

Chapter 39

Over the months after losing Josh, my mom's condition continued to deteriorate. I would visit her in the nursing home, and she seemed to get weaker every time. I decided to bring her to the house for the Fourth of July and have her stay all night. I picked her up from the nursing home and realized shortly after getting to the house that she wasn't going to be able to stay all night. She was so weak we barely got her in the house. Once she was in the chair, I knew she wouldn't be going outside for any fireworks or anything else. I called the nursing home and we ended up taking her back that evening. I felt horrible about it. I felt like I wasn't taking care of her and that I wasn't there for her. I had always been close to my mom, but the last few months, I had been selfish, and not available as much as I wanted to be.

The nursing home transported her to her doctor's appointments and I would meet her there. She had some tests to be done shortly after James and I were married, and we both went. She was very confused and all she talked about was wanting a maid-rite sandwich and a Pepsi. James went and got her both, and it made her so happy. She told me that day that I was a good daughter. I didn't feel like a good daughter. I felt like I had failed her.

Shortly after that appointment, we met with Hospice and decided to put her on it. She was very weak, and she had an open sore on her back that was being treated. She didn't talk much but would sing loudly, so the nursing home moved her to another unit. Her food became puréed and that bothered me. I wanted her to still have her Kentucky Fried Chicken, and I wanted my mom back. One day at the beginning of November, the Hospice nurses didn't think she had long to live. It was overwhelming. Before we lost Josh, she was still living in her apartment, talking to her friends, playing cards and all the things she enjoyed. How could things deteriorate so fast in a few months?

I went to visit her one night after they said she didn't have long to live, and her eyes were open, but I don't know how much she heard. I told her she was the best mom and how much I loved her. I told her that I wanted her to fight and live. Lily was pregnant and going to have a little girl. I knew how crazy Mom was about Lane and I wanted her to know her great-granddaughter. I told her that she needed to forgive anyone she has been angry with and that Jesus loved her. I told her that even though I wanted her to fight, I understood if she was done fighting. I understood if she was ready to leave this world. It hurt and the tears wouldn't stop, but she was suffering, and I couldn't be selfish.

Two days shy of six months from the time I lost Josh, I lost my mom. How could this happen? How could my heart handle anymore pain? How could I go to that funeral home and plan another funeral? I started going through Mom's stuff and found the documents where she wanted to be cremated and didn't want to have a funeral. I decided to have her cremated but I knew we also needed some closure so I planned her visitation and funeral the same as I did for Josh. Sitting in the same funeral home a few months after having Josh's funeral was devastating. Picking out another urn for my mom after picking one out for Josh only six months earlier tore my heart out. The guilt of not spending as much time with my mom as I wanted weighed heavily on me. When I was running around with guys that meant nothing to me, I should have been there for my mom. My grief kept me from spending those last few months with her. Yes, I visited her, but not like I should have. I can never get that back. The grief of losing Josh and then my mom was almost more than I could handle. But I put my focus on my husband, my kids, my grandson, and soon to be granddaughter.

It was also hard on my kids. They were all close to their grandmother. I was an adult and felt like an orphan and felt like my kids were left without grandparents. My dad passed away in 2012 and my mom in 2017. There was a different kind of grief knowing my kids would be without my parents and that my grandkids wouldn't know them.

Chapter 40

Moving Michael to a new school proved to be a mistake. He went from a very small rural school to a large school that didn't have the personal touch he was used to. He got in with the wrong crowd and had a lot of behavior issues. James's kids were grown, and he was already dealing with my grief, and coming into a family that had a lot of pain. Dealing with Michael's behaviors was a full-time stressor, and they didn't always see eye to eye.

Mike wanted to play baseball, so James bought him everything he needed. He wanted to bowl, so we put him in a bowling league. Mike was still in therapy, and he had a psychiatrist for his med management. His behaviors continued to escalate, and I was terrified he was going to hurt himself. He was running away from home, not doing homework, destroying things in our house, starting fires, carving names into his skin with pencil, and sneaking phones and tablets, adding Snapchat accounts. He had a lot of confusion from the abuse and it caused him to act out. He told the juvenile officer that he didn't care about anything or what happened to him. He spent a night in a detention center, and it didn't faze him.

As he got older, his behaviors became harder to handle. Before we lost Josh, and during the time I was a single mom, the men from church would spend time with Michael, and take him hunting or come talk to him when his behavior was out of control. One day, he jumped out of his window and was running down the highway. Josh threw on his boots and chased him down the road and brought him back home. He continued to destroy his stuff, so Josh moved everything but his bed into the dining room. Thankfully, I had a big dining room! Mike would listen to Josh, but when he was mad, he would also say mean things to Josh and blame him for stuff. One time, when he was mad at me, he said, "I wish Dad was here instead of you."

That hurt and I turned around and walked into my room before I started crying. I know he didn't mean the things he said. He was young and the sexual abuse he suffered was horrible. I just wish he could have seen how much we loved him and wanted him to be okay.

Journal entry September 9. 2015

My next issue is Michael. I don't know how to handle him. He is completely defiant to me and he talks back so much. He is doing bad in school and hasn't passed a book report yet. I know part of it is on me because I have no patience with him. Lord, please forgive me and help me to be a better mother to him. Help him to listen, be respectful, and help him to desire to do his schoolwork and help him do better in school. Lord, my whole family needs you. I worry about each of my kids so much.

I knew living in a bigger town wasn't the answer and we decided to move to a smaller town nearby. In the meantime, I was trying to reach out for help for Michael. I called so many residential centers, camps, homes, and so forth. No one would take him, or it would be so expensive I couldn't even think about affording it. About the time we found a house to rent in a nearby town, we got word that Michael got into a Christian place that had house parents and a private school.

We still moved to a smaller town, and we took Michael to Heartland. It was extremely hard leaving him but a relief to get him some help. I was terrified he would hurt himself or someone else. I couldn't lose another child. The first few months, he seemed to be doing great and I was happy to see the positive changes. They were good to him and communicated well with me. After several months, he started having behavior issues at school and was purposely failing his sophomore year in hopes that he would get to come home. Ten months after living there, Mike ran away from there. He was found, but he insisted that if he had to go back, he would run away again. I had no choice but to bring him home. Part of me was excited to have him back home with me and part was afraid he would revert to his old behaviors.

During one of the times we were having issues with Mike, Ray called Lily and she told him that we were having struggles with Michael. Ray blamed me for moving him, for getting married, and so forth. I'm not going to say I made the right decisions when it came to Michael, but most of his behaviors was from the trauma of the sexual abuse. Lily was very upset with Ray and hung up on him.

Since he had run away again, children's division was involved. We continued therapy and he had a caseworker. We had a good summer and I felt like things were going well. I caught him doing some things he shouldn't, but he was a sixteen-year-old boy, and I didn't expect him to be perfect. He seemed to take consequences and I thought that was a positive change.

He started setting up Amazon accounts and ordering jewelry for girls. I would cancel the accounts, but he would then sneak something else. When school started, he decided he wanted to do cross-country and I was so happy that he wanted to get involved at school. We took him and bought good shoes and would take him to practice at five in the morning. It was important to me to encourage positive behavior.

James and Mike seemed to get along better, and James was trying very hard to make a connection with him. July 29th, I tested positive for COVID-19 and James tested positive shortly after. We were quarantined at home and Mike was put on quarantine too. James ordered him a pitching net so he could at least go into the yard and have something to do. We played games, watched movies, and seemed to get through quarantine closer. A couple of months before this, Mike's children division worker asked if we should close his file since he seemed to be doing well. I asked her to keep it open until after school started, and now wonder if that was the best decision.

Shortly after school started, Mike got in trouble, and he wasn't taking consequences as easily. It was a Saturday evening, and we had both grandkids for the night. Mike was mad because we found out about him sneaking a girl into the house when we weren't home. He had a horrible attitude and things escalated. He threatened to run away, and I told him that he knew that if he ran away, I would have to call children's division. He didn't care. He was angry. James and he got into an argument, so I tried to talk to Michael. He was too angry to talk to. I wanted him to stay home and calm down, but he physically pushed me and held onto me. I ended up letting him go and he ran away. I called his children's division worker and she said that I would need to call the law. I also called Lily and Tony since the kids were here and they were scared because of Michael's behavior. I called the law and Michael returned shortly after and right before Lily and Tony arrived. Michael still had a horrible attitude when the officer arrived. The School Resource Officer also showed up and things calmed down. The following Monday, the juvenile officer came over and told Mike that if he ran away again, he would be taken somewhere.

Michael's school had some COVID cases, and he had to stay home a few days. I had a talk with him. I told him how proud I was of him and how much I loved him. I explained that I didn't want him to be taken away. I wanted him to enjoy high school, be a normal teenager, have a good life. I thought it was a great conversation. I blamed Ray for his behavior, but also knew that Mike must make the decision about how he is going to live his life. I didn't want what happened to him to define how he lived his life. Michael told me that he knew he deserved to be grounded and that he would take his consequence.

A few days later, I came home from work early and his phone was on the couch, but Mike wasn't home. He left his phone at home, so I couldn't track his location. I had no idea if he had run away again since he had a pattern of doing that. I called his caseworker. Michael came home after a bit and said he was just at the park. I had driven by the park and I knew he hadn't been there. He had no respect for any rules or me. All I asked of him was to be honest with me, respect the rules, and do his homework. I never asked him to have good grades, but to only do his best.

The following week, I came home and caught him using his school Chromebook to message a girl since he was grounded from his home laptop. I told him that I thought we had recently had a good conversation. He crossed his arms and looked at me with pure hatred and said, "Do you think anything you or anyone says to me actually gets through to me? I DON'T CARE!"

I left and headed back to work. I knew he had a cross-country meet that day and didn't want to fight with him. He was going to walk the few blocks to school to get on the bus. I was sitting at work when my phone rang, and it was his coach saying he never got on the bus. She was going to drive around and look for him. She didn't find him and ended up calling the cops. The officer called me, and I was already on my way home. It was a twenty-minute drive. I messaged a friend of mine and she had seen him earlier with a girl. She called the girl since her daughter was friends with her and found out the police had already picked him up. I didn't receive a call from the police station, so I headed straight there.

The officer met me outside and asked me how long it would take to get to Salisbury. I was racking my brain trying to figure out what was in Salisbury. He told me the cross-country meet was in Salisbury. It was at least a two hour round trip from my house.

I know I must have had a ludicrous look on my face. "Why in the heck would I drive him to Salisbury when he didn't get on the bus?"

The officer explained that the rest of the team would have to forfeit if Mike didn't show up. I know now that I should have said no, but I didn't want the team to forfeit because of Mike's behaviors. We went inside the police station where the juvenile officer, another police officer, and Mike were, and he was having a poor attitude. He didn't want to go to the meet. He had that "I don't care" attitude. They started giving him the speech we had heard a million times about life in detention centers. The life he would lead if he kept getting in trouble. Honestly, he can probably recite it word for word. I can remember the second time he ran away, and an officer talked to him, came out, and told me that he had really gotten through to Michael. I just looked at him and hoped he was right. He brought Michael out and told me that Michael was going to do his homework and do what he was supposed to do.

Michael looked at him and said, "No, I'm not going to do my homework."

The officer looked from him to me and was in shock. I wanted to say I told you so, but there is always that part of me that hopes that someone can get through to Michael.

After the speech we had heard a million times, I took Mike to his cross-country meet. I dropped him off, went to Casey's General Store to get a drink and go to the bathroom, and came back to pick him up. We didn't talk much. I didn't know until the next day that he was disrespectful and almost got into a fight with another member of the team.

I took Mike to his early morning practice the next day and found out later that he was disrespectful to his coach. At some point, he destroyed his cell phone so I couldn't know his location.

Chapter 41

We had a trip planned to go to Tennessee for Labor Day weekend and social distance with the family in the Smoky Mountains. We were leaving early Friday morning. Thursday morning at work, the SRO called me and said that Michael had acted disrespectful at practice that morning and that they were going to take him somewhere. I asked if they could wait until we got back from Tennessee. I wanted Michael to go with us. He said they worried that he would run away from us in Tennessee and didn't want to take that chance. I was an emotional wreck but went on about my day at work.

Later, I got a call from the juvenile officer that they wouldn't be taking him because they couldn't find a place to take him because of COVID-19. My emotions were all over the place. I had to change tactics and plan for him to go to Tennessee with us as planned. I had spoken to his therapist and he sent a letter to children's division stating that he needed residential treatment where he could get daily therapy. Scott had always been adamant about Mike staying at home, so I knew that he realized his behaviors were escalating. We have been told that Mike has depression, ADHD, and detachment disorder. Therapy is very important, especially with the trauma he experienced.

James and I both got home from work early to get stuff ready for the trip. Mike didn't come home after school, so I called the juvenile officer. She told me that she had just got off the phone with the judge and that they were taking Michael in about twenty minutes. Mike came home shortly after the call and I didn't say anything to him about them coming to get him because I didn't want him to run away. The children's division worker and the juvenile officer came to the house to pick him up and he didn't seem fazed. They told me they were taking him to a foster home and would transfer him to a residential center the next day. I hugged him tightly and once again felt my heart break. But I also felt relief knowing that he was getting help.

It was hard for me to go to Tennessee without him, but I knew the whole family was looking forward to it. The grandkids were excited. On Friday, I found out that they decided to leave him in the foster home until he went to court on Wednesday. On Sunday evening, after we got back to our cabin, Mike called me and asked me to come to Pigeon Forge to see him. I asked why he was in Tennessee and he told me that the foster parent he was with took him on a road trip over several states. I was not happy. We couldn't take him to Tennessee because of their fear of him running away but he was able to travel all over with a foster parent.

Chapter 42

Tuesday afternoon, the juvenile officer came by the house, and she didn't know about the road trip. She understood why I was upset. She said the judge would probably order residential care, especially since they have a letter from his therapist. I didn't want him to be in a residential center, but in my heart, I knew that was what he needed. If it was a year of his life to help him with his future, then it would be worth it. I was scared for my son. I loved him so much and wanted him to get help.

On Wednesday, I arrived at the courthouse a little early. I was talking to Mike, and he told me that he wouldn't be going to residential care but a different foster home. The juvenile officer, children's division worker, and current foster parent were around the corner talking. I walked around the corner and asked them why the plan changed. They said they wanted to start with the least restrictive plan first and keep him in foster care for now. So, the judge ordered him in foster care with the stipulation that if he messed up, he would go into residential care. I knew it was a mistake, but no one would listen to me.

I started to learn quickly that being on the other side of the system wasn't good even when a child wasn't taken from their home because of abuse or neglect but because of their behavior. I had only seen Mike twice since he went into care and that was two dentist appointments. The second appointment I took him to, he told me that he went for a run and that a girl called him hot, so he stopped and talked to her. He told me that he added her on Snapchat. I told him he was almost seventeen and a girl in seventh grade was way too young. He said she was fifteen. I asked him how he added her to Snapchat and he said he used the other boy's phone in the foster home. During that visit, he made it sound like the foster parents didn't care what he did. I mentioned it to the children's division worker because it concerned me. I have spent every day trying to protect him and that's what I was doing. At the Family Support Team meeting, Mike said he never told me any of that. He made it sound like I had made it all up. I was shocked, but then again, why should I be shocked? This was his behavior, but I kept hearing how good he was doing in the foster home. I hate that my son has learned how to be a perfect manipulator. But, when I think of the example he had as a father, what should I expect?

After a few months in care, Michael requested supervised visits and his new therapist, who never spoke to me, agreed. He requested these because he says I want him to fail and that I am negative. I believe he requested them because it is a control thing. Mike always said he wanted to be in control and didn't want people telling him what to do.

I have no desire for him to fail. I want him to succeed. I have spent nights without sleep worrying that he was going to hurt himself or someone else. I have tried to do everything I can to protect him and now he wants nothing to do with me. It is grief all over again. The sad part was that he was failing several classes, but they kept saying he was doing well in school. He needed therapy at least weekly, but he was only seeing a therapist every other week, sometimes less. His new therapist never requested records from his past therapist he had for five years. She never spoke to me or his siblings. She only knew what he told her. As a nurse, I have worked in mental health for several years and I know the importance of having the past records to get a full rounded picture.

I hope I'm wrong. I hope Mike succeeds. I would rather eat my words and him do well, than him fail. I love that kid more than he will ever know. I want the best for him, and if that means that he is happier in another home without me, than that is where he needs to be. I hope he looks back someday and realizes that everything I have done has been for him and his safety. I am here when he is ready, but I won't push him to be here. It is such an irony that Ray is in prison and doesn't have to pay child support, because he has no income, but they were quick to come after me for it when he went in state custody. I don't have any issues supporting my son, but I would rather do it directly for him then give money to the state.

As of July 2021, Mike is in a residential facility. Several months ago in court, he told the judge he wanted my rights terminated and wanted his foster family to adopt him. Shortly after that, he was moved because he was running away, getting suspended at school, being disrespectful, and failing school. When we went to the court, I told the judge that we wasted six months of time of him being in a foster home and not getting the constant therapy and help he has needed for years; the help I had been begging for.

After Mike moved to the residential facility, he decided he wanted to be around me again. I went there for a visit and therapy session by myself, James took me one time, and I had a virtual therapy session due to the distance. In our last therapy session, his therapist said Mike feels like he is the only one trying and making progress and the rest of the family isn't. Mike agreed with that statement, but I feel like that was put in his head from the way his therapist stated it. Mike is upset because he can't always reach Lily and feels like none of us come to visit him enough. The first time I went, I took him to lunch, and we had a good day. Currently, his level has decreased due to a running away incident and other things and he can't leave the facility. The place he is at has recently changed a lot of staff, and the therapist said that there were some staff members that are no longer there, that was the cause of Mike running away. I want to believe that he is trying and has made some changes, but I am skeptical.

He will be eighteen in December, and we have been dealing with these behaviors since he was eleven. I know how many times he has made people believe he was changing. Maybe my skepticism plays a role in me not trying as hard as he would like. I want him to heal. I want to restore our relationship. I love him more than he knows.

I received an email from his therapist last week that Mike no longer wants to communicate with us or have therapy sessions because we aren't trying, and he feels it isn't good for his mental health. It hurt. It hurt bad. I was hoping we were on our way to restoring our relationship. I was even picturing him coming home soon. I miss him but I will give him the space he needs to grow and heal. Hopefully, someday, he will realize that I am always here for him and that his family loves him so much.

I rarely hear from anyone. I respect what a hard job it is to work for children's services and the juvenile office. But I am shocked how easy it is for them to overlook parents who didn't abuse or neglect their kids. When we did foster care, it seemed like they catered to parents who had done horrible things to their kids. I'm far from a perfect parent, but I have done everything I can to give my children a good life despite what we have been through. I hope and pray Mike realizes that someday.

Update and journal entry from September 13, 2021

Court was difficult this morning. It is always difficult seeing Mike and knowing he wants nothing to do with me. It was weird seeing an ankle bracelet on him and knowing he is on probation. Why does he continue to run away? I'm not happy they put him back in that same foster home he started in. I'm mad that I have no say. Just frustrated. He told the judge he wants me out of everything and at least the judge told him he will realize someday that he needs a mom. The sad part is that the only reason he wants me out of his life is because he doesn't believe I'm in his corner. What?? Like seriously. I have always been in his corner. I have made my share of mistakes. What parent hasn't. But I've always told him how much I love him, how smart he is, how capable he is of doing whatever he wants with his life. I don't want what Ray did to him to define his behavior. It is days like today that make me even angrier with Ray and what he did to my kids. I was glad the judge told him he can't keep blaming other people for his behaviors and that he was heading down a hard path with his behaviors. He will be eighteen in a couple of months, and I have to realize that he won't be home anytime soon. The judge said he wouldn't force us down each other's throats and that it will probably be when we can talk to each other like adults to repair our relationship. When will that be? I miss him so much. I now realize that I am going to have to respect his choices and hopefully he will realize that I am here when he is ready. But that doesn't mean it doesn't hurt. I hate how he thinks I don't think he is capable of being good. Maybe because I know him better than anyone. I know how easily he manipulates. I know how good he can be at being good and pretending like he will do what he is supposed to. But I also know that he truly does have a big heart and he is funny and personable. Lord, I pray that he will realize what a good person he is. I pray he finds his way back to me someday. I pray that I can look at my own faults and be a better mother.

Chapter 43

February 14, 2021

Valentine's Day was on a Sunday this year. Both the grandkids stayed all night with James and me Saturday night. James's parents came over for lunch on Sunday. It was freezing cold, and more ice and snow was on the way. I had my second COVID vaccination in January and ever since I had severe arm pain. I had an appointment on Monday to get a steroid shot. After James's parents left, he planned to take the grandkids to meet Lily. I wasn't planning on going, but he told me to ride along. I complained but decided to go. When we were loading the kids into the car, our landlord was there. We had called him earlier to let him know that the bathroom pipes had frozen. We told him our dog Thunder was in his kennel and the house was unlocked for him.

It was a thirty-minute drive to meet Lily. On the way back, my phone rang. It was a Facebook Messenger call from our neighbor across the street. She told me our house was on fire. We were in shock. I called Lily and Devyn and I remember Devyn crying and saying, "Why does stuff keep happening to us?"

We pulled up to our street and there were firefighters and police officers everywhere. Our house was in flames. We were devastated sitting in the car watching firefighters work hard to try and save it. Ice was frozen to any exposed skin and their suits were frozen stiff. They worked hard but it was a loss. I kept thinking about all my stuff I had kept in the cabinet in the living room. All of my favorite things from Josh, his urn, my mom's urn, things James and I had collected since we had been married, and more. It was heartbreaking grief.

We found out that our landlord was trying to thaw out the pipes under our bathroom and left the house with the propane torch still on under the house. He says he turned it off, but our neighbor across the street saw smoke and went to the house and threw it out from under the house after turning it off. To us, the how and what doesn't matter, it is the loss.

After we talked to the fire marshal, went through all the procedures we headed to the town where James's parents lived and went to Walmart. We bought underwear, socks, a bra, personal items for a shower, clothes for the next day and other toiletries and was shocked that it was over four hundred dollars for enough stuff to get through a day.

When we left Walmart, I remember thinking I either needed to laugh or cry. I did both over the next few days, but at that moment, I needed a laugh.

"Happy Valentine's Day. And thanks for the new underwear. How did you know I wanted sensible, comfy panties?"

James replied, "Welcome, baby. Love you."

Chapter 44

The Blessings

We were very blessed and fortunate after the fire. We were able to find a house to rent the same night of the fire. We were able to stay with James's parents until we had stuff to move in. James's parents are great. I'm not sure how we would have got through many things without them. Feeling like an adult orphan, I am grateful I got in-laws who make me feel like I have parents.

We had rental insurance and so many wonderful people donated money, time, furniture, clothes and more. My sister is a clearance shopper and helped us to find a lot of bargains, plus she supplied us with a lot of household items and clothes. She helped paint in the rental house and spent time making sure we had everything we needed. I'm thankful for her and glad she is not only my sister, but one of my best friends.

It broke our hearts to lose our cat, Jack. They pulled Thunder out while he was in his kennel. He was upset and broke out of his kennel and ran back into the house. I think he was trying to find us. Thunder suffered severe burns but lived. He spent a couple of weeks at the vet, and they took really good care of him. Thunder is a red Boston Terrier, and his fur was so pretty. He still doesn't have all of it back and I don't know if he will, but he is back to being the heathen he was before, so we are happy! All of his vet bills were paid by people who donated to the vet office for his care.

I lost "puppy." It was in my cabinet and had been Josh's favorite toy. The firefighters did pull out Josh and my mom's urns. They were really charred but we were able to buy new urns and the funeral home in the town we live in moved the ashes to the new urns and didn't charge us. They also pulled out the Bible that Josh had with him the night he committed suicide. The Bible case was burned some, but the pages of the Bible were okay. That Bible is one of the most precious things of Josh's that I had left, knowing he had it with him that day. I don't look in it much. Even though it was thoroughly cleaned, there are pages stained with Josh's blood.

Chapter 45

Grief

Grief comes in all shapes and sizes, and it is very personal. No one can tell you how to experience grief, even someone who has been through the same type of loss. We are all different and experience that loss differently. Don't judge someone for still feeling grief for years to come. Don't judge someone for continuously posting their grief on social media. That may be what they need to do to find healing. Don't push someone by telling them the best way to get over something is to get back out there and live. They will live when they are ready.

Be supportive, be a friend, and let the person grieve. Yes, step in when they are doing something harmful to themselves or others, but otherwise let them grieve how they feel they need to. Don't put a deadline on someone's grief.

Grief comes from different situations. I had grief over accepting what my husband did and accepting that what we had wasn't real and was completely over. I have grief over losing not one, but two sons. Yes, Michael's loss is a different grief. I know he is alive and healthy, but I still grieve that he isn't with me. The grief of losing Josh is sometimes all-consuming. I have grief over losing my mom and my dad several years earlier. I have grief over the house fire and losing so many precious things that I can't ever replace, but I also saw the blessings that came through the pain.

I don't and won't ever apologize for my grief and how I have handled it. I have made my mistakes, and I have done things I regret, but I can't apologize for something so personal, and I wouldn't expect anyone to apologize or minimize their grief.

Chapter 46

The Light is still there
It wasn't hiding from me.
I hid from it
I was scared to grasp on to it.
If I opened to the Light
I would have to give up the anger
I would have to let go of the fear
I would have to give up the pain.
The Light is stronger than the darkness
Stronger than the grief
Stronger than the pain
I will grasp the Light as if my life depends on it
Because it does

Six years ago, my life was turned upside down when I found out I had been married to a monster for almost eighteen years. Everything in my life changed. I made mistakes, lots of them, but my love for my children never wavered. I didn't know what Ray was capable of which means that I was unable to protect them from the evil he perpetrated against them. Losing Josh almost destroyed me. Battling Michael's behaviors and the grief and hurt I feel over him not wanting to be around me tears at my heart every moment of every day. But I keep going. I have a husband who loves me more than I thought possible. The great part is that he isn't perfect, not even close, but that is what makes him so real. He isn't pretending to be the perfect husband or perfect father. I had that way too long. I think our biggest challenge is that James doesn't know how to handle my grief. He wants to fix it, but grief isn't something you can fix. It is personal and individualized. There are going to be days that I fall apart, and days I am upset because of grief. I have told James I just need him to support me in those moments; not get upset or try to fix it. It is unfixable.

Lily is married with two beautiful children and is a wonderful mother. She finally realized she is better not having any contact with Ray. I know she still struggles from the abuse, our family breaking up, losing Josh, and Mike, but she has a big heart and is a good person. We both know that when we call each other or text each other and say we need to talk, we are quick to say that it isn't anything bad! I am thankful for our close relationship.

Bailey graduated from the University of Missouri and works as a nurse near Chicago and was married in June. Bailey and I had some distance between us after everything happened. She had a lot of grief too. I was scared and didn't know where my place was after Ray and I divorced. In my eyes, she would always be my daughter. She was two when we got married and lived with us, but she also had her mom. I was scared of overstepping my place, so I stepped back. We had a good talk before her wedding, and I apologized for my part in the distance created over the years. I missed her and was thankful we were able to get back on track. We never used the word "step" when the kids were little. She always called me mom. Now I get to be "bonus mom" and I am happy to be in her life.

I know the wedding was difficult for her, knowing that Ray wasn't going to be there. She wouldn't have a dad to walk her down the aisle or have a father/daughter dance with. Those things will be hard for Devyn too.

Devyn graduated from the University of Missouri and works with people who have autism. She plans to get her master's degree next year and work with kids as a therapist. She is my "mini me" yet so much stronger and confident than I ever was. I love when she sends me random text messages saying, "I miss you." She is twenty-two, works full-time, has great friends, and is busy. I enjoy when we have our time together, even it is just lunch, or shopping.

I remember trying to make Devyn's last two years of high school memorable for her. I took her to a Justin Bieber concert and we had a blast, even though we had the very worst nosebleed seats. It was all I could afford, but it didn't matter to her. After she graduated, we were still in a lot of pain from losing Josh, but the two of us drove to Galveston, Texas and spent a few days celebrating her graduation.

Each of my children handled their grief differently and that is how it should be. They may be at different points in the process of forgiveness and deciding what part Ray will play in their future. No one should judge them for how they handle any type of relationship with Ray, whether they never want to see him again, or they talk to him periodically.

In 2010, I took a break from nursing and worked as a reporter. I had to go back to work as a nurse, and I love my job, but my desire is to be a writer. During all of this pain our family suffered, I graduated with a Bachelor's in English and Creative Writing with Concentration in

Fiction Writing. I am currently working on my MFA and have a 4.0. I want to be an author. I just turned fifty, but still young enough to follow my dreams. I plan to be a fiction writer and blend genres between mystery, suspense, and romance. I believe a good book will be well-rounded with strong characters. Now that I have completed this memoir, I can focus on my fiction writing, creating my website under my pseudonym, and following my dream.

I am happy and our life is good. We have overcome more than I ever thought possible. I made many mistakes as I fumbled through grief. I had grief over losing Ray, grief over what happened to my kids, grief over watching my kids hurt, grief over losing Josh, grief over Michael not being with me, and grief over memories that hurt. There are different types of grief and people handle them differently.

Life has been painful. The grief never leaves my side. It is a constant companion. My story isn't over as I am still dealing with issues with Michael and a system that doesn't really listen to the truth. My faith was shattered, and I turned my back on God, but thankfully, He is a forgiving God and loves me unconditionally. He has forgiven me, and I am finding my way back to Him and learning to trust again.

James and I have found a great church and a wonderful church family that I am crazy about. It was important to find a church that would accept James as he is, and we did. I wanted a church that would pray for him to know Jesus, and let God do the work in his heart. Our pastor and his wife have six kids, and I swear James is one of their buddies! He respects our pastor, the people at our church, and loves taking our grandkids to church. I believe that God brought us to this church.

I know I still haven't fully surrendered myself to God. I still hold on to fear that as soon as I trust Him something else will go wrong. My mind knows that it doesn't work that way. My heart just has a hard time catching up. There are people that God grabs a hold of, and their life is immediately different. For me, I am gradually growing back in my faith. That doesn't mean that God doesn't have a hold of me. It means that I am still holding on to that fear. God is and has always been there. He is waiting for me to find my way back, and I am working my way back to Him.

I am thankful and grateful for everything I have in my life. My best advice is to not let anyone tell you how to grieve and don't judge yourself for mistakes you make. You're human, you're hurting, and that is okay. Talk to loved ones, check on them all the time, don't think something can't happen in your family, and love yourself for who you are. Don't be afraid to ask the hard question, "Are you thinking about hurting yourself?" "Are you considering suicide?" It doesn't matter how you word it, it is important to not be afraid to ask the hard questions. No matter what you do, realize that life is worth living. I wish Josh would have realized. I wish he was here today.

"And once the storm is over, you won't remember how you made it through, how you managed to survive. You won't even be sure, whether the storm is really over. But one thing is certain. When you come out of the storm, you won't be the same person who walked in." -Haruki Murakami

Acknowledgements

I want to give a big shout out to my husband for supporting me through all my crazy moods and writing stress. He has the biggest heart, and I am grateful it is mine. He loves his kids more than they know, accepts my crazy family as his own, and loves his grandkids to the ends of the earth.

This book wouldn't be possible without the support and love of my children. They encouraged me every step of the way as I put this memoir together and I am grateful for who they are. I love each of you!

I have a fantastic mother and father-in-law, a crazy sister who loves big hugs (not really), and wonderful friends that have supported me on this journey. Thank you!

Pictured with "puppy"

Puppy fell apart many times!

Christmas when he was little

Our last Christmas with him

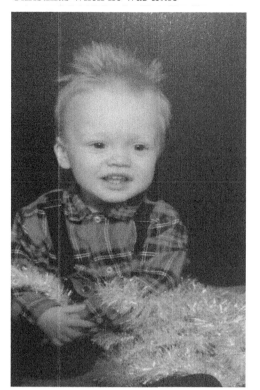

Holding Lane

In his element

Made in the USA
Middletown, DE
01 November 2021